Blood on the Canvas

The Life & Legacy of Boxing Icon, Canto "TNT" Robledo

by
Joseph C. Robledo

Golden
Foothills
PRESS

Published by Golden Foothills Press
www.GoldenFoothillsPress.com

ISBN 13-978-0-9969632-5-1

Cover photo: "Two Professional Boxers Boxing on Black, Smoky
        Background." ID: 675061423. www.shutterstock.com. (Modified by
        changing colors and refocusing faces.)
Book design: Thelma T. Reyna
Cover design: Thelma T. Reyna & Dom Gilormini
Printed in the United States of America

First Edition: 2018

Dedicated to the memory of my father,
CANTO "TNT" ROBLEDO,
who fought tirelessly to build meaning and purpose
in others' lives as well as in his own

Praise for Canto Robledo

"Growing up as I did in a boxing-rich family in Southern California, Canto Robledo was a respected household name. My father, Jimmy Lennon, Sr., recounted to me his many accomplishments in the ring and his great popularity. Moreover, I personally came to admire Mr. Robledo in his later years as a deeply caring man and a remarkable trainer with quite a story to tell!"

--Jimmy Lennon, Jr
Professional Boxing Events Announcer

"Canto Robledo was a great inspiration to the sport of boxing, showing what dedication and strength you need not only to be a boxer, but a manager and trainer, no matter what handicaps you have."

--Danny "Little Red" Lopez
World Boxing Council World Featherweight Champion, 1976

"Canto was a happy-go-lucky guy with a perpetual smile. Always giving and helping the community. A civic leader and an assist to boxing."

--Jack Mosley, Trainer:
Father of "Sugar" Shane Mosley
World Boxing Council World Welterweight Champion*

"It took me a while to understand Canto, at first. I thought he could see a little bit. He was telling me things that appeared to me that he could see. How does he know that? He's blind, I would think....He was afraid of nothing; it was like he wasn't blind.... The 'Man upstairs' guided me straight to Canto and I truly thank Him. All I have accomplished was a result of Canto coming into my life, and I truly loved him."

--Dargin McWhorter
Golden Gloves Champion Lightweight Division: Johnson City, TN
Colored Golden Gloves Champion Lightweight Division: Chattanooga, TN

"For over 55 years, Canto Robledo trained young men in his gym and joined them at the boxing venues of Southern California, such as the Olympic Auditorium ... without the advantage of sight. His sense of hearing and sense of touch were acute, and the aid of his assistants was valuable. In addition to working with boxers in his gym, he put on dances, shows and benefits at local schools and halls regularly. He worked closely with the community leaders of Pasadena to do what he could to help....Canto Robledo is remembered as an 'icon' among Pasadena community members."

--Peter Embody
Longtime Personal Friend

"From Canto I learned the magic of perseverance....The key element that set Canto Robledo apart from any other person that I have known is character.... When you reach a point in your life when you can step forward and do what it takes to get the job done, then you have character. Canto had more character in his little finger than many of us have in our whole body. Canto rose to the occasion. Indeed, he did."

--Joe Rodriguez
National Junior College Lightweight Champion
Ring Announcer, Pasadena Arena

---

* Other titles won by Sugar Shane Mosley were: International Boxing Association World Super Welterweight Champion; World Boxing Association Super Welterweight Champion; World Boxing Council World Super Welterweight Champion; World Boxing Council International Champion; and International Boxing Federation World Lightweight Champion.

AUTHOR'S FOREWORD:
Childhood Memories

My fondest memories of my father began at an early age. Before I was born, Canto had been blinded at the age of 20 in a boxing ring during one of his matches. I can remember my father when I was a young child, gently touching my face, shoulders, arms and legs, rubbing his fingertips across my eyebrows, nose, mouth, and ears. I didn't realize, until I was about five or six years old, that he couldn't see me. I understood later that Canto had only wished he could see me and was using his tender, fatherly hands as his "eyes" to see his youngest child.

When I was playing on the kitchen floor, and I saw my father coming in my direction, I would have to move, or he would accidentally step on me. I learned to move my toys quickly out of his way, so he wouldn't trip and fall and sometimes step on the toys. My mother, Concha, trained us children to keep ourselves and our home safe for the sake of our father. Even so, I never felt that our household was different from others; I felt like we had a normal home.

My father walked with his arm stretched outward, bent slightly, so he would not run into doors, cabinets, or walls. I don't remember him using a cane to get around. Oftentimes, he relied on my mother, brother, sisters, and me by putting his right hand on our shoulders as he navigated his way around. My father wanted to be as independent as possible, but as I grew older, I learned to put his hand on my right shoulder to lead him around in places with crowds.

Even though he could not see, my father was conscientiously the protector of our family. Before going to bed, he always checked the knobs on the stove to make sure the gas was off, checked the water faucets to make sure they were not leaking, checked the locks on the windows and doors, and made sure the telephone was properly on the hook. When bedtime came, he would come to our bedsides, kneel beside our beds, and say prayers or recite the rosary.

I enjoyed spending time with my father because he taught me many things about life and boxing. He understood that I was eager to learn. He would sit me on his lap, put one hand on my shoulder to measure distance, and tell me to make a "fist" and "throw a jab" into the palm of his hand. I was about five years old when I learned my first right hook.

When my father established his boxing gym in the backyard of his father's home—which is where he lived early in his marriage as he was adapting to his blindness—many people wondered how a blind man could teach boxing to others. Canto had a keen sense of touch, keen hearing, and clear mental imaging of his surroundings. He taught boys how to box by standing behind them and placing his hands over their shoulders, arms, and legs. In this manner, he could ascertain if their stance was correct, if the punches were being thrown correctly, and how much power the trainee was using. He also had his assistants—brothers, friends, visitors, or formal trainers—describe to him verbally how the particular trainee stood, threw jabs, and moved around. From these descriptions, Canto knew what needed to be corrected, and he gave instructions for this.

It was during my childhood that I began a routine to box and train in our gym. My father devoted many hours in the gym teaching me the proper techniques of the sport. For example, turning the left hand when an opponent is striking. Footwork was also essential, especially keeping my balance while punching with both hands. He taught me how to learn from my mistakes. If I forgot to keep my hands up and dropped them unthinkingly to my sides, he would tap my shoulder with the trainers' hand pads as a reminder.

My father always enjoyed exercise and liked to take walks. Sometimes he and I took long walks around the Rose Bowl sports complex in Pasadena, which has a three-mile perimeter. It was on these walks that I learned the most about my father. I was in high school, and we developed a very close bond during this time. I listened closely to his advice and gained insight into his perspectives on life. He referred to these as *consejos*, which means *advice*.

Canto instilled in me a deep resolve never to give up and to persevere to the end, whatever the task or challenge was. He consistently encouraged me to be strong and courageous and to be a positive role model. I also learned from him to listen to others, which allowed me to understand people and to be compassionate toward my fellow human beings.

Did I ever wonder what it might have been like to have a father that could see? No. I accepted my father just as he was. Watching him train all the young boys and young men who came to his gym, seeking his guidance to become professionals, or to be champions in their age divisions, or simply to be stronger, gave me great joy and delight. It was inspiring to me, and I myself aspired to be a boxer and attained that dream, as did all the trainees who came to Canto's Crown City Boxing Stables for many decades. I became a Golden Gloves champion in my adolescence simply because of the teaching and inspiration my father gave me.

My mother, Concha, was my father's eyes and his primary rock of support. She was the only driver in the family, chauffeuring him around town and out of town for his many boxing shows after his blindness. But my father had many friends and relatives that willingly stepped forward to do what they could for him, whether it was helping him build his gym, or running his fundraisers at his Stables and in the community, or driving him places. The old proverb, "You reap what you sow," applied to Canto: he gave love and assistance to others, treating others with respect and valuing them, and, in turn, he was consistently shown kindness and respect.

I grew up enjoying the boxing business under my father's guidance and mentorship until my adulthood. Who knows what kind of a life he would have had if he had not been blinded? I know for certain that I probably would have missed a lot of the meaningful life experiences we had together. I was blessed to have had such a wise, insightful, and inspirational father.

That is why, when I retired after 38 years of teaching, I committed to writing this book, to describe the legacy of my father in his amazing life of 88 years, including his six decades of giving back to the community he loved so much in Pasadena, California and beyond. His incredible story demonstrates how a man dealing with a major physical shortcoming is able to overcome constraints to fulfill dreams that might seem unattainable. The guiding light in Canto's life was his wife and partner, Concha, who exerted uncountable efforts in helping Canto to face his doubts and prevail.

My father and mother were a dynamic team, with an incredible love story of lifelong devotion to one another and to helping others, especially disadvantaged youth. I was truly blessed to be their son.

--Joseph C. Robledo

INTRODUCTION

by Rick Farris
President, West Coast Boxing Hall of Fame

I'll never forget the first time I saw him. It was 1965, a Friday evening at the Teamsters Boxing Gym in downtown Los Angeles.

It was a night of Junior Golden Gloves competition, and I was scheduled to fight in a novice match. I'd heard of the blind boxing trainer, Canto Robledo, and had seen him on TV working the corner of his boxers. But that Friday night, when I saw him on the arm of his guide, I forgot all about my own upcoming bout.

There was something different about his presence. Beyond having no eyesight, an almost palpable energy seemed to surround him. People would approach him, boxing people, the fighters, the trainers. He was soft-spoken, but his words were strong and direct, with calm control. Canto made no attempt to hide the eyes he could no longer use.

I asked my trainer, Johnny Flores, about Canto.

"Did he lose his sight boxing?"

"Yes," Johnny replied. "Canto Robledo fought some of the best in the world. He fought out of Pasadena when I was a kid. At the time, there were a lot of great Filipino fighters here, in addition to the great Mexicans and the rest. Canto fought them all ... Speedy Dado, Young Tommy, Clever Sencio, and more."

Johnny told how Canto had some defeats as well as his many victories. "However," Johnny said, "the fights he lost were all close. In his sixth pro fight, he defeated a future world champion, Chalky Wright."

I wanted to know more about Canto Robledo, and during the next half-century, I slowly put together pieces of the historic boxing career of this very special man. As things turned out, I faced a couple of Canto's boxers in amateur competitions, and they were always tough, so Canto was a familiar boxing figure to me.

One day, in the summer of 1970, shortly after my pro debut, I saw Canto at the Main Street Gym. It was a Saturday morning. Later, my stablemate, heavyweight contender and eventual champion Jerry Quarry, was going to be sparring with one of the best young heavyweights on the West Coast, Wayne Kindred, one of the best heavyweights in Canto's stables.

Canto was on the gym floor, right by the big mirror near the entrance where I was about to skip rope. I approached him and said, "Hi, Canto." The blind trainer turned his head to face me.

"Hello, Ricky," he said calmly. How could he have known it was me? I had walked up from behind him.

I stepped closer, and he, amazingly, appeared to see me stepping closer to him. As I was about to take his hand in mine, Canto touched my shoulder, leaned forward, and spoke genially to me. I will never forget his energy. I suddenly understood how he could teach boxing. I understood the secret: it went beyond eyesight. It was instinctive, a sense beyond the physical sense of merely seeing. It was real, not just a myth.

During the Golden Era of professional boxing, Canto Robledo was one of the best in the world. However, Canto's true gift from God, his enduring legacy, was his incredible teaching, his influencing, his guiding of others under his tutelage. To this day, years after his passing, he is still here, still teaching. His spirit and energy, his heart and soul of a champion, live on. For this and for all the caring, wisdom, and love he embodied, the West Coast Boxing Hall of Fame is proud to honor Canto Robledo!

CHAPTERS

CHAPTER 1:
He's Tough, Won't Go Down

The bell sounded for the first round. Both fighters rushed to the center of the ring and proceeded to pummel each other with powerful, attacking blows. Canto "TNT" Robledo, a rising young Pacific Coast Bantamweight Champion from California with 41 fights under his belt, including 25 wins, 11 losses, and 5 draws, was the favorite. He soon took the lead with two quick left jabs to the head and right crosses to Hilo Hernandez' jaw. Hernandez was a respected boxer in the United States and had 11 wins, 5 losses, and 1 draw.

Hernandez counter-punched with left hooks and right crosses to Canto's head. Canto finished the round with an impressive flurry of blows that sent his opponent back on his heels and stumbling to his corner. In the second round, Hernandez unleashed an aggressive attack of combinations, but Canto countered with punishing blows to the body and took control of the fight again.

Canto controlled the fourth and fifth rounds, but at the end of the fifth, he was cut above the right eye. The bell clanged to end the round. Canto stepped quickly to his corner as soon as his trainer placed the stool down, and Canto's manager, Tom Donahue, ducked through the ropes. He noticed his boxer's cut above the right eye, which was now bleeding profusely. The corner man, Otto, tended to Canto's ominous-looking laceration.

"You're getting to him!" said Donahue. "Hear that crowd, Canto? They love it!"

"He's tough, won't go down," Canto replied.

"Keep pouring it on, Kid, another couple of rounds," Donahue urged.

"You should lay back," added Otto, "and watch the eye."

"I'm running this corner," Donahue barked in the din of the crowd. "We can't lay back, you dummy! We need a big win tonight, so go get him, Canto, you hear me?"

The referee ordered Donahue out of the corner. Canto nodded his head and moved out quickly at the bell. The battle continued with neither man giving space. Canto pressed too hard and too carelessly. He scored with a solid body and head combination that buckled Hernandez' knees, but near the end of the round, Canto was stunned and dazed by a terrific left hook on the temple close to the cut. Again blood gushed from Canto's eye and down his face. He had trouble seeing out of the eye, then was rocked again with a powerful left hook directly on the eye.

Stunned, Canto simply stood there, shaken, knees sagging. Mercifully, the bell clanged to end the round, and Canto walked shakily toward his corner. Donahue rushed out to guide him to his stool, throwing water at Canto, whose eyes began blinking. The trainer scrambled between the ropes to tend to the cut with a gauze pad but noticed that Canto's right eye was unmoving.

"He can't see!" Otto yelled.

"Sure he can," Donahue shouted at Otto. "What the hell's wrong with you? Get back outside the ropes!" Then to Canto: "You're all right, aren't you, Canto? We've got to win this fight!"

"All right," Canto muttered.

"Stop the fight!" Otto screamed at Donahue.

"Are you crazy?" growled Donahue. "That would wreck everything!"

Otto re-entered the corner of the ring and urged Canto: "Keep your hands high above your eyes!"

Donahue pressed on Canto's eye with the gauze pad. He poured water on him again, and worked frantically, helping him to breathe deeply while barking instructions to him.

At the start bell, Canto moved cautiously to the center of the ring, then hesitated. Hilo Hernandez moved in and fired several combinations to Canto's chin and right eye. The boxers clinched, and Hernandez pushed off, striking Canto with the left elbow above the right eye. Unchecked, Hernandez continued to use dirty tactics by thumbing Canto in both eyes, but the fight continued. Canto, summoning his will, determination, and fighting power, went on the attack. This enabled him to stay in the fight, holding onto the lead he had gained in the earlier rounds.

But Canto's vision was fading, darkness creeping into his line of sight. He thought to himself: *I must knock him out with a strong left jab, then a left uppercut and a powerful right cross.* He stood in the middle of the ring, wet gloves by his side, sweat dripping down his face. Canto's confusion argued with him in his swirling head: *What's wrong? I just threw a hard left hook and a crushing right cross. It caught Hilo on the jaw and he's down. Why is the crowd booing? What's going on? Why are they throwing cups in the ring? They seem to be booing ME! Why isn't the ref counting him out? The bastard keeps thumbing me in the eyes, not once but several times.*

Stunned but still standing, Canto's thoughts raced: *Oh, my eyes! Why are they blurred? Burning with hot sweat! Can't see clearly, just shadows. What's happening? Got him with a solid combination. He's down, or is he?*

"Canto, what the hell did you hit me for?" blurted the referee as he stood close to the boxer.

Canto said, "I didn't know I hit you, Ref. I thought you were Hilo."

"Don't let it happen again. Next time you'll be disqualified, understand?"

"The guy keeps thumbing me in the eyes," pleaded Canto. "Watch him!"

"OK," the referee said. "No harm done. Just keep it a clean fight."

Canto's eyes were hurting and stinging, with nothing in focus. The images in front of him were blurred, but at least he could make these out, even if they weren't clear. *I've got to get this fight over with. I've got to knock this kid out now!* Canto thought to himself. As Hernandez rushed Canto, Canto pounded his right glove on Hernandez' jaw, and this time, it was Hernandez who went down for the count, not the referee.

The referee counted to eight, and Hilo Hernandez rebounded to his feet. Despite his failing vision, Canto fought hard, his will to win keeping him upright till the end of the round. In his corner, Canto told Otto that he couldn't see clearly, and his eyes were burning. He could only see shadows, he said, and asked Otto to rinse out his eyes. He was having trouble seeing the right hook. Otto poured water over his eyes to clean them out, but still Canto couldn't see clearly.

"We need to stop the fight if you can't see clearly," Otto told Canto. "Your eyesight's much more important than winning!"

But because of his steely desire to win, Canto refused to disappoint the crowd. He insisted on staying in the ring, despite severe pain, and vision in both eyes now almost all gone.

Because of Canto's natural instincts and boxing skills, he was able to block and counter-punch Hernandez' powerful blows. The fight finally ended with Canto victorious in a split decision. He had won the fight! Pandemonium broke loose at ringside, with people rushing the ring, wanting to congratulate him. His handlers and trainers scurried to his side, whooping joyfully, "You did it! You did it, Champ!"

Canto needed to get away as quickly as possible. "Hurry! Get me to the dressing room!" he said through gritted teeth. "Hold my arm. I'm seeing spots and sparks. Everything's getting darker. Don't let the press near me! Get me back to the locker room!"

Away from the crowds, Canto lay confused and concerned on the rub-down table, while Otto and Tom Donahue tried to reassure him.

"Don't worry. We'll get you to a doctor right away. You'll be fine," said Otto.

"The doctor's one of the best in town. He's a good friend of mine," Donahue interjected. Then, after a pause:

"And don't worry. He won't report this problem to the boxing commission. Don't worry. You'll be ready in three weeks for the big title fight."

CHAPTER 2:
The Robledo Family's Early Years

What brought my father Canto to this match, this boxing ring in California that fateful night that everything went dark for him? The trials and suffering that Canto's life was just beginning to endure had begun like many journeys of Mexican boxers who found acclaim in the United States for their skills and achievements: as a child of an immigrant.

Canto's father Felipe and mother Soledad, my brave grandparents who were among my first heroes, had escaped the dangers of the Mexican Revolution of the early 1900's, a very challenging, dangerous time for the Robledos as well as for their homeland. My grandparents had wanted a safer, better life for their family, and they needed to move quickly, especially after one harrowing encounter when Soledad was home alone with her children.

One evening, while Soledad was starting to cook dinner for her family, loud thumps on her home's old wooden door startled her and the children. Felipe was away, and Soledad was caring for her two toddlers, Benny and Manuel. Cautiously, she opened the door slightly and saw armed men standing on the other side. They pushed their way into the house, demanded food and water, and assured her that they would not harm her or her family. Frightened and worried, Soledad quickly cooked food for them and served them as they commandeered the old wooden benches and chairs in her poor home. It was obvious these men were looking for young boys whom they could kidnap to fight in the Mexican Revolution. Though she was not harmed, Soledad was shaken and fearful for her family's future. She and her husband must start preparing their departure from the nation they loved but that was now enmeshed in revolution.

Within weeks, Canto's parents and their children embarked upon their trek to America. Soledad was pregnant with their third child, so the family was traveling with her midwife, a friend of hers, at her side. One day, as they stopped to rest along this journey, Soledad went into labor for over eight hours. It was a hard delivery, but the family's third child emerged healthy and wailing energetically. Canto, my father, was born. When Felipe heard the baby's cries, he broke into a large, happy, relieved grin. The day was January 19, 1913.

My grandparents, Felipe and Soledad, expanded the Robledo family like clockwork as the years passed. They had migrated to the United States to work in the fields, following the crops from region to region, month to month, as nature dictated that crops ripen. They had come to America in their horse-drawn wagon, which they had used in Mexico for traveling. Now, safely here, they used this wagon to take Felipe, his wife, and their children from field to field throughout the Southwest: to Colton and Beaumont in California, for example, and to Tyrone, New Mexico again, my father's birthplace.

Felipe's journey to America had been fraught with danger: road bandits, other predators, limited resources that forced Felipe and his family to camp out in the open, even sleeping in the shelter of a boxcar. Not speaking English, Felipe and his family faced cultural challenges as well as challenges navigating the rules, places, and expectations of surviving. Journeying to California, then journeying from town to town, and to other states, following the crops as migrant workers, was hard on Felipe but also on his entire family. After the birth of my father as their third child, my grandparents had expanded their traveling family with two other sons, one of whom died at the age of one.

But the tradition of Mexican itinerant workers went back many generations. Felipe and Soledad knew clearly what type of life they'd have as itinerant laborers. They were grateful for their work, despite the strenuous toll it took on their bodies. Felipe learned to speak and understand English quickly, knowing that transiency of work locations required reliable communication. The children adapted to the flux of their lives. They kept themselves entertained by using sticks and an occasional ball to play with. They played with other children at the various camps and villages that they passed through or lived briefly in. They were also integral in pitching in however they could with their parents in doing work in the fields and elsewhere.

Felipe was a highly resourceful man who didn't limit himself to laboring in fields. He was constantly on the lookout for jobs as he traveled throughout the state in their wagon. Once, he sold shaved ice cones, called "raspas," or "shavings," to make ends meet. He also worked in coal mines in New Mexico, served as a police officer briefly in that state, and worked in a copper mine. Felipe's work ethic was rigorous and a point of pride for him. He cared deeply about supporting his family to the fullest extent, and, with his deep faith in God, he knew his family would survive and thrive.

Felipe, Soledad, and their children eventually decided to settle in California in 1921, had two more sons, then moved in 1922 to the beautiful city of Pasadena as their final destination. Three more children expanded my grandparents' close-knit family. Having arrived in America with two children in tow, now Felipe and Soledad faced challenges with seven children. They had chosen Pasadena as their landing place because they had several relatives living there, thus giving his family a place to live. In one relative's house, my grandparents' family was so cramped, they had to sleep on the floor "lined up like cigarettes," they said. Children were told to go outside and play and not come back until suppertime to avoid crowding the house all day.

Felipe became a skillful gardener and found employment at the famed Busch Gardens for many years. Later he worked as a gardener at the Thornton Estate in San Marino, a small city tucked to the south of Pasadena and known for its high level of wealthy residents. He also learned barber skills and worked at this craft for many years. His talents were seemingly endless, fueled as they were by a phenomenal work ethic and devotion to his family's well-being.

৵৵

Canto as a Young Man: A Budding Boxer

Early on, Canto Robledo showed glimpses of physical traits that would in the future lead to his fame as a boxer. He was versatile in various sports—soccer, tennis, baseball, track and field—and had amazing agility, being able to move gracefully and quickly from side to side. He had quick feet and large, heavy, fast hands. His sense of balance was acute. He excelled in athletics, earning certificates in all his sports. If his hands ever hit you, playfully or in athletic competition, it would hurt because of their strength and speed. Canto enjoyed playing sports. He was not a large kid physically, but he established a reputation of being a natural athlete who was talented in many ways.

He loved academics and was considered a good student, always engaged in class. He was playful, active, spirited, and dedicated to doing well. His honors began when he was only 10 years old and won a certificate in track and field by placing first in the soccer ball distance throw. Soon thereafter, at the age of 13, he won the City Championship in Tennis, in Senior Doubles. His quickness in moving sideways, with superb balance, and having fast hands helped him be a tennis champion, as these would later help mold him as a boxing champion as well.

Even though Canto did very well in school scholastically and athletically, because of his small stature, he was targeted. Tough guys often bullied him. They would throw fruit, cans, and rocks at him, punched him out of meanness, and laughed at him. Canto tried to appease bullies by offering them his lunch, but they socked him and took his lunch anyway. He withstood their punishment and protected himself against their assaults as he would do, years later, as a boxer in the ring: he kept his hands up and his chin down.

But as time passed, Canto became frustrated by the bullying and by being unable to overpower the attackers. He wanted to learn how to protect himself better. His father Felipe, a fan of boxing, taught him how to hit a heavy punching bag with an old pair of boxing gloves he'd somehow acquired, and he made Canto spar with his brothers. Then, one day, when a bully came at him, Canto blocked his blows with his left arm and swung his right fist into the mouth of the tough guy. The bully yelled, his nose bleeding, and ran away. Canto felt a surge of confidence, and he knew that fighting back physically to protect himself from injury and mockery was the only way he'd get these bullies off his back.

❧❧

A Girl Named Concha

On a bright, early, sunny day, Canto and his older brother were headed to Sierra Madre to pick oranges at a ranch just northeast of Pasadena. Canto's brother, Benny Robledo, a tall, handsome man with a wide grin and neatly combed, straight black hair, served as an independent agent who provided local workers from around Pasadena to pick oranges at the ranch and supervised them in their work. Benny recruited laborers from surrounding cities, including Sierra Madre, Monrovia, and Duarte, as well as Pasadena. Riding in a 1926 flatbed truck, Benny made morning rounds to collect the workers, including teenagers like his brother Canto who were anxious to work. The crew usually included Charlie and Manuel Jimenez from an area known as La Manda Park in East Pasadena. Benny once mentioned to Canto that this Jimenez family had eight sisters, and they were all very beautiful.

Canto was about 15 at this time, developing a work ethic like his father's, focused on helping the family to thrive. Growing into manhood now, he had a clear vision of what this entailed, and he accepted responsibilities proudly.

But work was only one thing on his mind as Canto approached manhood. One day, in Benny's truck on his way to harvest fruit, they stopped to pick up the Jimenez brothers, Charlie and Manuel. Canto's eye was caught by a lovely girl he saw hanging laundry on a clothesline in the Jimenez yard. She had long, flowing black hair, captivating eyes, and the most adorable smile Canto had ever seen. She was one of the Jimenez girls, one of the vaunted eight sisters Benny had mentioned to him. When the topic is pretty girls, news spread fast.

At first the girl didn't even notice Canto, but something in her heart must have told her to look toward the truck. Her eyes met Canto's, and he waved at her with a big grin on his face. The lovely young girl, 14 years old at the time, was named Concha. She blushed, smiled, and returned his wave. She was fascinated by this handsome young man named Canto.

Concha attended Jefferson Junior High School and walked to school daily with her sisters, Mary, Nora, and Chole. When they arrived at school one day, the girls saw posters in the hallway announcing the upcoming annual spring dance. This year's theme was, "Blue Moon Garden Dance." The poster exhorted: "Come early, dance, and have a great time."

The excited girls wondered if they would be able to attend. Concha found herself hoping that one of Canto's brothers would invite him to the school dance, since he was not a student there, but his brothers were. Blushing, Concha felt eager to see Canto again.

Concha's Family: Coming to America

Concha's family, the Jimenez family, had humble beginnings, dangerous challenges, and life-changing struggles in Mexico, like the Robledo family had also suffered. The Jimenez family emigrated to the United States with great risk as they sought a better life, as the Robledos had. And, like the Robledos, they had fled their native land fearfully during the Mexican Revolution, when Pancho Villa's army raided small towns, stealing food, money, jewels, horses, and livestock. They also stole the pretty daughters for their pleasure as well as forced young men they encountered to fight in their rebel army. As a result of the terror and upheavals of this civil war, the Jimenez family had fled across the border.

They journeyed from Nuevas, Chihuahua, Mexico to El Paso, Texas, then on to Fierro, New Mexico, where my maternal grandfather, Jose Jimenez, found work in the iron mines. Grandmother Jimenez recalled years later the hard times they had, with the children sharing shoes and clothes, often going barefooted when this survival trick didn't work. She described harsh winters heating their simple house with a pot-belly stove. One day, Concha's sister Mary got too close to the open-flame stove and her dress caught fire. Her parents rolled her on the floor in a blanket until the fire was out. This was a frightening event for the family.

But despite the hard times, they made the best of it. When the opportunity arose to move to Pasadena, California, the Jimenez family had packed up and eagerly left New Mexico. During their journey to Pasadena, they had stopped in farming towns to rest. Grandmother

Maria was not too happy about farm life and told my grandfather she'd had enough of it. Learning to drive their ox cart had been the last straw for her! She and the whole family looked forward to living in a city.

꿍꿍

Lighting the Flame of Love

About two months after Canto and Concha had locked eyes and smiles as Canto sat in Benny's truck, Canto and brothers Benny, Manuel, and Julio arrived at the "Blue Moon Garden Dance." They were neatly dressed, Canto in black pants, white shirt with a tie, a top-coat to match, and black wing-tip shoes with a nice polish. In fact, Canto had made it a point to spit-shine his shoes for the dance, making them amazingly lustrous and sharp-looking. Canto felt that this was his big opportunity to catch the lovely Concha's attention and, hopefully, to impress her. Though he wasn't sure that she would be in attendance, he felt pretty sure that she would indeed be there. His heart beat fast in anticipation.

Concha noticed Canto looking remarkably handsome, when he entered with his brothers. He noticed Concha standing with her sisters next to the refreshment table. The young girls were talking, drinking fruit punch, and giggling to themselves. Concha had her eyes on Canto and wondered if he would ask her to dance. Her young heart fluttered, filled with excitement and nervousness. Canto walked slowly, with an air of confidence, over to Concha and asked her to dance. She said yes. They began to dance and talk, and she hung on his every word, eager to know more about him.

As the hours passed, the couple was seemingly oblivious to the others present at the dance, caught up as they were with one another. By night's end, Canto and Concha had developed a powerful connection. They made plans to see each other again and did so at another big event. The city of Pasadena was hosting a big band musical at its popular Memorial Park band shell. Most of the Robledo and Jimenez siblings were there. This was an exciting time for Canto and Concha to continue getting to know one another in their budding romance.

They went off together to talk, Canto holding Concha's hand tenderly as they strolled through the park. He was very optimistic about his boxing career and shared his goals with her. He told her that he was going to fight as a professional boxer. He was very serious, very resolute about his plans, and she felt his passion. She expressed support for his dreams and hoped she'd be part of his success in attaining them.

After several months of their courtship, Canto wanted to express his honoring of Concha and his affection for her by meeting her parents, as is common in the Mexican tradition. He got his chance to do so at a "Jamaica" held one lovely spring afternoon. Canto noticed Concha arriving with her sisters, mother and father, greeting the other families they knew who were already there. Canto wanted to make a good impression on both parents. He waited for the right moment to approach them. With a big smile, he walked over to Mr. and Mrs. Jimenez and introduced himself.

He extended his hand to them and said smoothly, "It's a real pleasure to meet you." Just then, Mr. and Mrs. Robledo came over to greet the Jimenez family. This made Canto and Concha very proud and happy. Canto had completed one of the tasks a young man in love needed to fulfill.

The fiesta had folkloric dancers, a Mariachi band, and dozens of food and game booths, along with a red and white wine-tasting stand. The annual fiesta was a big hit with the public and a great fundraiser for a local church. One of the highlights of the day was the crowning of the fiesta queen, a gorgeous local girl who graciously thanked the attendees and gave them her best wishes. The priest blessed her and said a prayer for the families gathered together in celebration of their religious community. As night fell, a colorful piñata was strung up on a line from one end of a tree to another, with someone holding the line and controlling the height and movement of the piñata as children took turns swinging at it, with the children organized in line from smallest to tallest. Blindfolded with a colorful bandana, each child took a turn swinging exuberantly at the candy-filled piñata to crack it open and be the hero of the day. Amidst cheering and exhortations to swing the piñata stick this way or that, the children persisted until the colorful paper piñata eventually gave way to so many blows and expelled its contents on the ground. When the piñata broke, children and bigger kids scampered to collect the candy and bubble gum scattered all over into their paper bags for this occasion. This was the special ending to an evening of camaraderie and getting together under the stars.

◈◈

The love between Canto and Concha blossomed and deepened as the months and years passed. They had been so young when they'd first met, and now adulthood was approaching. Concha would occasionally sneak out during the day to meet Canto at the corner phone booth. They would hold hands, share a soda, and speak about the fun things in their lives, such as school, family, special outings, important events going on at home and in their neighborhoods. Invariably, at some point before parting ways, Canto would kiss her on the cheek and gaze at her soulful brown eyes.

"I love you, Concha," he would profess.

His heart was on fire for her.

"I love you, too," she'd say in reply each time. But each time Canto heard her declaration of love for him, it sounded as fresh and exciting as the first time she had said this.

"I only want the best for you," he said. "I picture us together, with me providing comfort and a good life for you."

She smiled. "And for our kids?" she would ask coyly.

They'd laugh and hug. They often discussed what their life together would be like, and, yes, it always included children. Canto described to her what his vision was for them: him winning boxing matches, her in the audience cheering him on, and him coming home with a nice paycheck for his victories. He wanted so much to be a champion boxer, not just for his own satisfaction, but for the sake of being a good provider for his wife and future family. His father had made a big impact on Canto as a stalwart man who did whatever it took—taking odd jobs here and there, learning new skills wherever he went—in order to provide well for his family.

For her part, Concha felt that Canto was special. He was determined and resilient with awesome courage. Everyone knew about Canto in Pasadena. He was well-liked and respected by friends, neighbors, and family. He was also very handsome. She often counted herself lucky that the person she loved was not only a man of deep, spiritual values and character, but a very handsome one, too.

Above all, Canto was a protector. Once bullied and deprived of his lunches in the school yard, Canto had now evolved into a young man who worked hard to be healthy, fit, and strong. One day, as he waited for Concha at the corner phone booth, a tough-talking guy with red, dirty hair and freckles asked him, "Who are you waiting for, punk?"

Canto was no longer someone who could be intimidated. He replied calmly, "My girl, Concha."

This particular bully was named Jimmy. He laughed and told Canto, "Well, she won't be your girl for long."

"Oh yeah?" said Canto.

"Yeah," said Jimmy. "I like her, too, and I'm coming between you, breaking you up, and taking her for myself."

With lightning speed and an accurate left-right combination, Canto struck Jimmy on the jaw. The arrogant, provocative Jimmy dropped to one knee, got up, mouth bleeding, and ran away.

CHAPTER 3:
A Dynamite Right Hook

One day at Brookside Park in Pasadena, Canto saw an older boy picking on a much smaller boy whom Canto knew. The older, bigger boy was getting the best of it when Canto came over and told him to stop hitting his friend.

"If I stop, I'll hit you instead," the bigger boy said.

Then he rushed Canto, who was slightly smaller than the bully, but Canto was ready for him. As the older boy swung at Canto with a left hook, Canto blocked the hook with his right hand then came out with a hard-left hook to the boy's jaw, followed by a dynamite right hook. The boy went down, screaming and crying in pain. He got up and ran away.

Canto felt a deep sense of satisfaction in facing a bully fearlessly and stopping him in his tracks. All the years of his own harassment at the hands of bullies throughout his school years flashed through his mind as he walked away, but he didn't have to worry about bullies anymore. The sparring his father made him do with the family's old boxing gloves at home, taking turns with his older brothers, had taught him something helpful. Canto knew how to defend himself, or his friends, against aggressors. Canto was an aspiring boxer, after all.

Unbeknownst to Canto, he had an audience watching the whole incident, from the arrival of the bully, to Canto's confrontation of him, to the final dust-up. This observer was named Morrie Cohan, and he had good reason to be so interested in the scuffle. He approached Canto.

"Hey, kid," said Morrie, just loud enough to get Canto's attention. "That was a great right hook. Where did you learn that combination?"

Canto said, "Oh, I learned to fight in the picking camps." He said nothing about his father. He looked the stranger over quizzically: "What's it to you?"

"Well, I'm in the boxing business," said Morrie, "and I like your style. How would you like to learn how to box properly?"

Canto replied, "You mean I don't know how to fight properly?"

"Hey, kid, you seem pretty good, but I could train you in boxing to make you a champ one day."

"How you going to do that?" asked Canto.

"Just come over to the Pasadena Arena, and I'll get you going. But first I have to get an okay from your parents. Where do you live?"

"687 Cypress Street," replied Canto.

"What time is your old man home?" asked Morrie.

"Mom is always home, and dad gets home after dark."

Morrie nodded his head and said amicably: "OK, I will see you at the Arena around 9."

❧❧

The Pasadena Arena

After picking oranges for a week, Canto and Benny decided to rest and relax. One day, Canto decided to visit the boxing gym, the Pasadena Arena, on south Fair Oaks Avenue. It was the middle of July, a hot summer day. Fifteen years old and eager to train, he absorbed all the sights and smells of the place. Several other boys and some men were training, hitting the heavy bag, getting their hands wrapped, shadow boxing in the mirror, sparring in the ring. A heavyweight boxer was jumping rope. The gym had that smell of sweat and cigar smoke in the background. Older men sat on benches watching the action from the viewing area, each one paying two cents to watch and talk about the new and upcoming prospects.

He was greeted by Morrie. "Good to see you, Canto. Come with me."

He took him to the corner of the gym where the heavy bags lined the wall. There was space to jump rope and two speed balls hung nearby. The boxing ring was in the center of the gym. Morrie handed Canto a pair of boxing trunks and told Canto to go to the locker room to change his clothes but leave his tennis shoes on. When Canto returned, Morrie took him over to a hanging punching bag and helped him wrap his hands and put on a pair of 16-ounce gloves.

"Now you're ready to begin," said Morrie. "Here comes the trainer who's going to show you the correct way to box. Listen to him and follow his instructions. He'll guide you in the right direction."

The trainer was of medium height, stocky, with a German accent, and with the biggest hands Canto had ever seen. Just looking at this guy put a feeling of anxiety in Canto, but it was quickly dissolved when the burly trainer broke out with a big, toothy smile.

"Hey, kid, my name is Otto," he said.

He was a middle-aged man who was brought up in the fight game. He had over 30 fights and a solid winning record when he retired due to too many broken noses and cut eyes.

"I'm going to teach you things that you don't know yet."

"Great!" said Canto.

"OK, kid," said Otto. "Let's see how good you are. Start punching the heavy bag."

Otto showed Canto how to stand, how to bob and weave, stay balanced, and mainly how to throw a left jab, then the one-two left hook. Canto was able to pick these movements up quickly and effortlessly. His punch was solid, smashing into the bag with determination and accuracy.

"Keep your hands up!" Otto barked. "Don't drop your left hand after you jab."

After 10 minutes of punching the heavy bag, Canto's arms tired, and he was sweating profusely, but Otto kept pushing him not to quit. The 10 minutes felt like hours to Canto. Thankfully, Otto finally said, "Kid, take a break. Go pee or drink some water."

Canto took the break, but when he returned, he was still sweating.

"Okay, let's move on!" said Otto.

Otto spent another half hour with Canto, showing him how to shadow box, how to hold his hands, and how to move his feet and hands at the same time. He was really getting tired, but Otto was just starting. Otto then took him over to an old speed ball looking deflated and worn out as it dangled from the ceiling, as if it would break at the first punch. Otto showed him how to use the ball, then said, "Okay, kid, now you do it."

Canto was a disaster with the speed ball, being so tired from all the other training he'd done. In his first swing, he missed the ball completely, but he soon got into a rhythm and was hitting the ball in smooth rat-a-tats.

Overall, Canto's first day at the Pasadena Arena was difficult. When he arrived home, his mother took one glance at him and declared, "You look so tired, my son."

"I am, and I think I'll take a nap before eating," replied Canto.

He went to bed and didn't awake till the next day. He felt refreshed and ready to go back to the gym. His mom had breakfast waiting. He gobbled it down and was out the door. When he arrived at the gym, Otto was not there yet, so Canto put on his trunks and shoes and was struggling to wrap his hands.

When Otto finally arrived, he saw Canto almost all ready to go and said, "Wow, you are an eager beaver! Let me help you with the hand wraps and gloves."

It was another grueling day of the same routine when they stopped. Canto asked, "When can I start sparring with a real guy?"

"You're not there yet, kid," said Otto. "I'll let you know when you're ready, so don't ask me anymore" He glanced at the disappointed boy. "You and I will both know when you're ready."

"What do I still have to learn?" asked Canto.

"You have to do some other things like road work, rope jumping, and changing your diet."

᪥᪥

For two weeks every day, Canto reported faithfully to the gym and worked out diligently, including the road work and other routines Otto had planned for him. Canto knew he was getting stronger and more confident. He felt he was ready one day when Otto told him to put on his sparring gloves, mouthpiece, as well as protective head gear. Canto was going to spar with "Young Duke," a local fighter with three amateur fights to his name, and an undefeated record. Young Duke was a Filipino from the Hawaiian Islands who was a tough cookie and could exchange punches at a fast-rapid pace. He had a straight, accurate, solid jab that could do substantial harm. His straight black hair was cut neatly, and he was a cool cat. Young Duke didn't speak to anyone except his trainer. He was a favorite in the gym, a good young prospect on the horizon. He was under contract to Morrie Cohan.

Canto was led to a boxing ring made from canvas flooring and rubber "ropes" that looked like old garden hoses tied together to form the "square circle," as the boxing ring is called in the sport. Young Duke was pretty much the same size and weight as Canto. Canto got into the ring, and Otto gave instructions to both.

"Now, when the bell rings, come out fighting and remember to keep your hands up."

The bell clanged, and Young Duke and Canto walked quickly to the center of the ring. Both threw a lot of missed punches and did a lot of clinching.

Otto yelled, "Keep your hands up, chin down, and keep jabbing!"

As the sparring session progressed, both fighters improved. When the bell finally rang to end the last round, Canto felt he had outboxed his opponent and felt he had won the sparring session. But Young Duke felt the same, so both boys raised their arms triumphantly.

In the dressing room, Canto proudly reflected on his first sparring session, thinking, *I like this sport. Maybe someday I can become a champion, with hard work, proper training and guidance. I know it is possible.*

❧❧

Months of training passed. Winter came and went, and spring had arrived. One day, Otto told Canto he had entered him in the Golden Gloves Boxing Tournament. Canto was excited and said, "I will win my first fight."

Otto told him he had three months of daily training to get ready. During that time, Canto did his road work around the perimeter of the Rose Bowl, running at least once a day and sometimes twice. As he got stronger, he found he had much more energy, more stamina, and more determination.

His cardiovascular fitness was remarkable. In the gym, Canto's training consisted of rope-jumping, working out with the speed ball, and punching the larger heavy bag. Canto sparred regularly with the various fighters in the gym, especially his two older brothers, Benny and Julio. Benny was a left-hander, which helped Canto increase his self-defense skills. Canto was now 5′ 6″ tall and weighed in at 116 pounds. He was required to see Doctor Goldwater, who oversaw the medical part of the examination regarding the tournament and praised his fitness.

Canto's father owned a Chevy and always made time to get Canto to all these events. Felipe and the entire family were extremely proud of Canto. Felipe, who was a demonstrative father, never afraid that showing tenderness and love to his beloved family would diminish his manliness, expressed his pride by putting his arms around his son, giving him a big hug, and telling him, "I love you, son, and I'm so proud of you. You're going to do great!"

◦⚬◦

In the summer of 1927, the big event—the Golden Gloves Boxing Tournament—was held at the Grand Olympic Auditorium in downtown Los Angeles. The Golden Gloves was one of LA's big events of the year. It was a full house that night, the air charged with excitement and thousands of fans' loud talking. The crowds bought the requisite hot dogs, peanuts, a cold beer or soda, and streamed to their seats, ready to cheer spectacular battles.

Canto was assigned to fight out of the blue corner and had to dress in the blue dressing room. There were three to five fighters in the blue room, all getting ready for their events. He was scheduled for the eighth bout of the evening, which meant he had a long resting period. He had his trunks and shoes on, and his hands were wrapped.

He started loosening up his body by stretching and shadow boxing. When he felt adequately warmed up, he sat down to contemplate the evening. He had completed a full year of rigorous training, and he was ready now. The time had dragged slowly for him the past year, with the hours upon hours of gym work, road work, and building himself up for this night. Finally, a tall, thin man with receding blond hair opened the door and yelled, "Eighth bout, let's go! You're next! "

Otto, his trainer, was with him and immediately held his gloves while Canto shoved his hands into them. Otto tied the gloves securely. Canto was now ready to go to the ring. He had a towel around his neck. The tall blond man returned and yelled again, "Let's go! You're on!"

Canto made his way out to the ring followed by Otto, Morrie Cohan, and his father Felipe, who seemed to be bursting with pride as he walked with his head held high. The walk to the ring seemed to be miles long to Canto. When he reached the ring steps, he went to his corner with Otto at his side. Canto did a bit of shadow boxing. The ring announcer introduced Canto in the blue corner, and Canto smiled, his hands up and waving to the crowd.

At the center of the ring, Canto and his opponent received instructions from the referee. These included orders to protect oneself always, no hitting below the belt, no thumbs to the eyes, no rabbit punches, and break when told to break. Then the referee stated, "Touch gloves and come out fighting!" Canto slipped the towel off his neck and, as he returned to the blue corner, he genuflected and gave himself the sign of the cross. God was with him. Now Canto was ready to fight. The bell clanged to start round one.

Canto could feel the excitement in the air and the blood rushing through his veins. The crowd was going crazy, yelling, cat- calling, whistling. The air was heavy with the pungent smell of cigars. The Olympic Auditorium was a packed house. The first blows of the fight were thrown, with Canto immediately peppering his opponent with a series of left jabs and right crosses. The opponent countered with a left hook and a right uppercut. The fight was on!

The bout went the full three rounds and then was over. The boxers waited for the decision, both young men anxious. Finally the bell rang for attention. The referee strode to the center of the ring to announce the result: Canto won with a split decision.

Canto was jubilant, jumping in the air. Felipe was in the ring first, hugging him, then lifting him off his feet. The crowd roared, and Canto had a huge grin on his face as he waved to the fans. Canto returned to the dressing room with his father, Otto, and Morrie, and found all his family members celebrating. They hugged and kissed Canto. When things quieted down, Otto told Canto he wanted him to go home and rest, as he was slated to fight his next opponent the following day. Canto followed orders and slept soundly.

❧❧

The second round of the Tournament had Canto matched against a rugged Mexican kid with a tough chin and solid boxing skills. Both fighters were in the bantamweight class and closely matched. This second bout went the full three rounds and was another split decision win for Canto.

The third and final match was on a Sunday. As expected, the Grand Olympic Auditorium was packed with standing-room only. Canto was assigned the tenth bout. The time seemed to drag slowly while he was waiting and preparing for his match. Finally, the thin, tall man with blonde receding hair made his entrance and yelled, "This is the main event for your weight class, and you are on!"

Canto entered the walkway leading to the ring, followed by Otto, Morrie, and Felipe, and quickly got into the ring. He was anxious and ready to go. The officials went through their routine announcements and introductions of celebrities in the audience. Both fighters were called to the center of the ring, where they were given the standard instructions then returned to their corners.

The first round was exciting. Both fighters pummeled each other, but Canto appeared stronger in the last 30 seconds of the round, where he continued to throw a "flock of gloves" at his opponent. The round ended with him pounding a five-punch combination, inflicting notable damage to the opponent. The bell rang and Canto returned to the corner, his face red but not bleeding.

In the second round, Canto was the aggressor from the outset. He peppered his opponent with the left jab, followed by a right cross. He let loose a punishing left hook and a solid right cross to the chin, dropping the opponent to the canvas, where he rolled over onto his back. The referee started his count and Canto retreated to his neutral corner. The opponent rose from the canvas, somewhat dazed, with a cut over his right eye and blood flowing from his nose. The bell clanged to end round two. Otto worked on Canto, wiping him down, giving him water and instructions as the bell sounded for the third and final round.

Canto let go with a stinging combination, a left uppercut with a dynamite right hook. He knocked out his opponent. The referee waved his hands to stop the fight. Canto won with his first knockout. The doctor on site revived the opponent with smelling salts. The crowd was on its feet, roaring, whistling, and throwing coins into the ring to show their appreciation and approval of both fighters. Canto learned that at the end of a fight, if the crowd throws coins into the ring, the amount collected off the canvas would be split 50/50 between the boxers. Both handlers gathered the coins on a towel and took them to be counted and distributed.

Felipe and Canto's entire family were at the fight. They all decided to celebrate Canto's win by going home and joining friends. It was a great night and the beginning of Canto's fight career.

A few days later, during one of Canto's workouts at the Pasadena Arena, Morrie approached Canto and told him that the city of Wilmington was having "smokers," an amateur boxing show at a night club. Of course, Canto would not be paid any money, but if he fought his ass off, he would get some Mulligan stew and a food certificate for $1. Canto agreed to take the fight.

Canto fought at five more smokers by the end of the year, winning all of them and feeling very confident in his improved boxing skills. On one occasion he even won a Timex wrist watch, which he gave to his father. His career was off and humming along nicely.

CHAPTER 4:
Turning Professional

In January 1929, Canto turned 16 and faced a moment of truth in his young life. He was at a crossroads where he had to decide about his career. He considered boxing his calling in life. He had a vision with Concha for the future, and that included boxing. After several months of training in the gym, he had realized that perhaps one day he could turn professional and earn a decent wage to support his own family. No longer did Canto want to toil in the spider-filled fields picking grapes and oranges. His picking days in the blazing summer sun were over.

Canto knew that Morrie Cohan could help guide his professional boxing career. Morrie was a boy promoter as the owner and operator of the famed Pasadena Arena. He had many business boxing connections that could help Canto become a ranked professional fighter.

The "Boy Promoter," as Morrie was known to boxing fans, was a clean-cut fellow, square as square could be, with a high degree of integrity. He enjoyed socializing with upper-class citizens in Pasadena where his weekly boxing shows were a smash hit. Morrie was responsible for many top professional prospects in the area. The "Boy Promoter" created champions.

Morrie would be able to manage Canto's pugilistic career. Canto understood that a professional fight is quite different from an amateur fight. First, the rounds are increased to four rounds instead of three. The lengths of the rounds are longer, from two minutes to three minutes, and there is no use of headgear. The size of the gloves was much smaller. To run and exercise and train every day was a necessity. Despite sore legs, exhausted arms, and tired feet, a professional boxer pushed on.

First Canto had to talk with his parents to get their permission for him to become a professional fighter. He could earn $2.00 a fight for four rounds, and more when he fought the main events. He knew he had the skills, talent, and courage to become something special, a warrior in the ring. Canto's parents were supportive of his decision to turn pro.

Canto signed a professional contract with Morrie. Canto felt comfortable with Otto as his trainer and suggested they sit down and talk. Canto informed Otto that he wanted him as his trainer for his professional debut. Otto agreed and told Canto that he must be dedicated to the fight game and be willing unconditionally to give it his all and abide by Otto's requirements.

Otto demanded that Canto's running routine must include running every day between five and eight miles around the Rose Bowl perimeter. Canto must train six days a week and rest on Sundays. In addition, he said Canto must follow a proper diet. Daily sparring would become routine. Canto would spar at least eight rounds, if possible, depending upon who the sparring partners were. At times, Canto and Otto would have to travel to Los Angeles to use the Main Street Gym for more sparring and training. This was a larger gym and was frequented by more professional fighters.

Morrie explained to Canto that the fight purse would be divided as such: one third for the manager and two thirds for the fighter. The trainer was paid from five percent of the fighter's share and five percent from the manager, for a total fee of ten percent of the purse. Morrie began to make plans. He wanted Canto to get a new professional mouthpiece, blue and white boxing trunks, and a pair of boxing shoes. He told Canto that he would purchase these items for Canto, then deduct the cost from his purse.

Turning Pro

In short time, Morrie scheduled professional bouts for Canto. The first was a four-rounder set for him to fight Johnny Gabucco at the Athletic Club on June 29, where Canto's pay, the "purse," would be two dollars. Canto was ready, feeling very confident and in great shape. He signed the contract, and the fight was set. This was the official beginning of Canto's professional career, with his hopes and dreams of becoming a champion now greatly strengthened. Otto and

Canto were excited and motivated to train even harder to get Canto into top shape. He would run twice a day around the Rose Bowl perimeter.

Canto was exuberant about the upcoming fight with Johnny Gabucco at the Main Street Athletic Club in Los Angeles. The Robledo family was thrilled for Canto but felt apprehensive about the bout, though they still fully supported Canto's new status as a pro. Canto wanted to impress Concha, the love of his life. He also saw the fight as merely a business opportunity to make money and help support the large Robledo family. Canto played it cool, and coolness is always a good trait to own when considering a future in boxing.

Canto won his first bout against Johnny Gabucco in a split decision. After the fight, Canto and his father went to the local diner and ordered ice cream with apple pie. After taking one bite of the pie, Canto realized that his jaw was too sore for him to eat his ice cream and pie. He gave all of his money to his father that night.

Canto continued to stay in shape and was ready for his next opponent. Morrie informed him that he would fight Regino Palmini in a four-round bout. This would be a four-round curtain-raiser at the Pasadena Arena, with the purse being two dollars. In what was considered a slow start, Canto warmed up a bit in the last two rounds, in which he was most impressive. He defeated Palmini and was now on a two-fight winning streak. He was still only 16 years old at this time but was beginning to experience some ring success, even making some good money. He was able to save enough money to buy Concha a promise ring.

Canto was happy and proud about the money he was earning in the fight game. He began buying food for the family and clothes for himself. He wanted to save enough money to buy a car, even though he did not have a driver's license. He regularly visited the Jimenez family and started going steady with Concha. They enjoyed dancing and going to baseball games at Brookside Park in Pasadena.

Morrie Cohan told Canto one day how impressed he was with his boxing abilities. He called Canto "a real crowd-pleaser." Morrie also discussed changing the spelling of Canto's last name from Robledo to "Robleto," to make it seem Filipino, because in the

Philippines, that is how the name is spelled. Morrie felt that this would enable Canto to fight more Filipino fighters and draw more of a Filipino crowd, which would translate to more money for Morrie and for everyone. There were many popular Filipino fighters in the fight scene in Pasadena at that time, and these fighters drew good-sized crowds. Some of these fighters were Foster Manalo, Young Tommy, Speedy Dado, Pedro Villa, Pete Sarmiento, Young Sport, Clever Sencio, and Sid Torres.

Morrie was a very smart businessman who knew how to please the public, which included controlling the press and attracting the Hollywood crowd. Canto also added "TNT" to his name, along with the change to "Robleto." These changes were noted by the press and proved to be attractive to boxing aficionados.

Canto fought another four-rounder at the Pasadena Arena on August 22, 1929. The purse was still two dollars. His opponent, a rough guy from San Bernardino named Jimmy Martinez, proved no match for Canto, who won by a unanimous decision in an impressive display of speed, power, and class. This was Canto's last fight as a pro contracted to Morrie Cohan, because Cohan's connections to the Pasadena Arena were becoming overwhelming, and he needed to change his focus.

Victories and Defeats

In these times of flux and hardship, all commercial enterprises experienced adjustments. Morrie decided to sell Canto's professional boxing contract to Tom Donahue, an established manager of several professional fighters. The offer that Donahue made for Canto was too lucrative for Morrie to reject. Canto was the first and only main event professional boxer in Donahue's stable, the "top dog" of the boxers.

Tom and Canto decided to take on the young, tough Foster Manalo from the Philippines. By this point, Canto's fame was spreading. He would star as the main event of the evening at the Pasadena Arena and would earn 100 dollars, the most money he had earned as a professional up to this point. Canto was impressive in his huge upset win over Foster Manalo at the Arena. The fight crowd was pleased with his performance in a sizzling eight-round contest. Canto was steadily rising in the flyweight division and was earning good pay. He enjoyed fighting at the Pasadena Arena, where all his fans and family could come and watch the fight. He was in terrific shape and continued to train hard.

One day, Tom informed Canto and Otto that Canto's next fight would be with a young, fast and talented Filipino fighter from Manila named Young Sport. This fighter had been making headlines in the fight game. He wanted to fight Canto in an eight-round bout at the Pasadena Arena on November 27, 1929. Canto tasted defeat for the first time in his budding professional career. Young Sport won on a split decision.

A rematch was scheduled. In the next bout, on December 12, 1929, Canto would once again lose to Young Sport in a close split decision. Both fighters put on a spectacular show for their fans, with each fighter pounding his rival's body with both left and right blows meant to wear down the opponent. In the fifth round, Canto threw his dynamite straight, right-hand punch and opened a cut on Young Sport's left eyebrow. Blood gushed out onto the canvas. Going into the last round, the fight was considered even. Young Sport happened to land the last blow and was impressive in the last 30 seconds of the round, which influenced the judges to give the decision to the Filipino. Both fighters had put on a fast, furious, memorable show.

This was Canto's second loss to Young Sport in back-to-back fights. The appreciative crowd showered the ring with pennies, nickels, and dimes. But Canto suffered a broken right hand in that match and did not receive proper treatment. He was told to just put the hand in a bucket of ice. Unfortunately, Canto abstained from fighting for one entire month.

On January 16, 1930, Canto would fight tough Johnny Navarro in Pasadena, just one month after his loss to Young Sport and coming off the training lost due to his broken hand. Many people felt these affected Canto in the bout, and he lost in a split decision to Navarro. One month later, on February 6, 1930, Canto took on Navarro once again at the Pasadena Arena and received a draw in the fight.

Despite his losses and draw, despite his injury and the pain he experienced, Canto wanted to continue to box and make money. Tom Donahue booked him to fight on March 6, 1930 against an experienced fighter named Johnny Jordan. Canto lost the match and was disqualified for hitting after the bell. Undaunted, Canto fought the following month against Emil Jure from San Bernardino to win a four-round decision.

As Canto's skills improved, he became "more hungry," as is oftentimes said of athletic competitors. He became more ambitious, more confident that he could continue rising to higher levels, earning more money and more acclaim.

CHAPTER 5:
Taking It to a Higher Level

Tom Donahue and Canto decided it was time to raise their game several notches, so they took on a highly regarded boxer known as Chalky Wright for an eight-round contest at the Pasadena Arena. Chalky was the favorite, but Canto defeated him, winning a unanimous decision over Wright on April 4, 1930. The following month, on May 8, 1930, Canto notched another victory, this time over Pedro Villa in another crowd-pleaser at the Pasadena Arena.

Canto continued to grow stronger and excel. Tom had offered him a chance to fight the famous Delos "Kid" Williams in a 10-round main event at the Arena. Williams, one of the best in his weight division, had battled all the major contenders. Canto would earn $100 for the contest, a fine sum of money, especially in the Depression. The fight took place on May 29, 1930. It was Canto's fifteenth fight, but Williams had about 40 fights to his credit. Canto was 17 years old at this time. Williams, a ranked world-class contender, was 22 years old.

Canto had to be very dedicated and in top physical shape for this match-up. This was his big chance to upset a prestigious favorite and would be a huge achievement for Canto as he rapidly ascended the ranks to the top of his game. Canto felt very confident but humble at the same time to be earning such an enviable opportunity to showcase his skills. After all, this was Canto's first major top contender, perhaps one of the best in the country at this flyweight class. He needed an upset of this nature to propel himself into the next level.

Canto fought his heart out to take a close decision from Delos "Kid" Williams in 10 spirited rounds. In later years, looking back on this milestone fight, Canto said it was around this time that his eyesight began to bother him slightly.

◈◈

A Bad Stretch for Canto in 1930

Canto had heard of Speedy Dado and had watched him work out at the Main Street Gym in Los Angeles. He felt strongly that this tough Filipino was someone he must defeat to continue his rise to the top of the game. Tom Donahue agreed.

Donahue scheduled a match with Dado in a 10-round battle at the Pasadena Arena on June 12, 1930. Dado would be the favorite in the fight, and Canto would earn $200 that night. Canto was very motivated and eager to meet Speedy Dado in the ring. Dado was always in excellent condition, so Canto knew he had to train twice as hard as he usually did to defeat this classy, hard-hitting Filipino. On the appointed night, before hundreds of fevered fans, the battle between the two talents unfolded and ended, 10 exciting rounds later, in a draw.

For two months after this popular fight, Canto rested and nursed injuries he sustained in the bout, as well as from the Kid Williams match-up. His hand had been injured again, and he had to rest it. Also, Canto's eyesight became problematic again. He used to tell me that he would see sparkles in his eyes at times, and that these flashy spots were very painful. He had a difficult time sleeping and suffered headaches as well.

After these two months of recuperation and reflection about his career and fighting the next opponent, Canto and Donahue decided it was time to fight again. This time it would be the mighty Midget Wolgast from New York. This would be one of Canto's biggest paydays, earning $2,000 for the bout; and, should he win, he'd get a shot at the world's title. After several days of negotiations and contract proposals, Tom was able to secure the fight at the Hollywood Legion Stadium. The contest was set for August 8, 1930.

It may have been a mistake in Canto's fighting career for him to take on the best contender the world had to offer at that time, but this was during the Great Depression: the huge payday was very attractive. In retrospect, our family wished he had not agreed to this fight. Midget Wolgast was older than Canto and had fought better fighters. He was on track to fight for the world's title in New York. Perhaps for Wolgast, fighting Canto was a so-called tune-up fight. He was a more experienced fighter than Canto and had defeated all the contenders in his weight class. Canto aimed to fight for the world title someday, and he had to go through Wolgast to earn it, even if it meant injuries to his eyes. This was his biggest chance for an upset, and Canto was willing to go for it all.

But Midget Wolgast was too much for Canto. His boxing experience was evident in the contest. Wolgast was a harder-hitting puncher and had a solid, tough chin. He was short in stature and could work his way into his opponent without being hit much. Wolgast's iron chin could take a good punch. He could pummel with either hand. Canto lost the lopsided bout on a 10-round decision.

Still stinging from this loss, Canto fought again the following month, on September 4, 1930. He was knocked out by Pete Sarmiento. Starting with the Speedy Dado match, Canto had now gone without a victory in three back-to-back fights. He'd been set back on his heels, as the saying goes. His knockout by Sarmiento was his first KO, and it did nothing for his confidence.

Going back to where he'd recently come closest to winning, his draw against Speedy Dado, Canto agreed to fight Dado again. Dado was still a respected boxer, the uncrowned champion of Hollywood. Once again, Canto fought to a draw against Dado at the Hollywood Legion Stadium, on October 31, 1930. This was the fourth straight match Canto had had in 1930 without a win. He wanted to fight again right away.

Tom Donahue agreed to schedule a fight on December 1, 1930 with "Young Sport," who recently had won two split decisions against Canto. This third match between the talented Filipino and Canto would be a 10-round main-event in Santa Ana, California. Again, Canto lost, this time to being disqualified for excessive holding and grabbing.

Canto had hit a bad stretch in his young career. He tried to keep in mind that he'd suffered injuries in two bouts that had stolen two months of rigorous training from him. Perhaps this involuntary time off had contributed to his losses, draws, and disqualifications. Canto needed to get back to winning. This year was a test of his willpower to continue pursuing his dreams. He was ready to put this challenging year behind him and get back in winning form.

&&*

Rising from Defeat, Winning Big

Canto would go on to fight 10 more times, winning all 10 of these bouts. He defeated Peppy Sanchez, Tony Atizado, Clever Sencio, Abie Israel (twice), Joe Calder, Johnny Jones, Sid Torres (twice) and Bobby Mars.

Next up was Speedy Dado again. Coming off a 10-match winning streak, Canto's confidence and fitness were much more solid than they'd been the last time he and Dado had met in the ring. In the Dreamland Auditorium in San Francisco on November 6, 1931, Canto won a split decision over Dado. With this he also clinched the Pacific Coast Bantamweight Title, reigning supreme in three states: California, Oregon, and Washington state.

As a newly-minted champion, Canto revisited other matches he had not won. He wanted to redeem himself, it seemed, to prove he was indeed a champion. A rematch with Young Sport was scheduled, and Canto defeated his old nemesis in a 10-round main-event spectacle at the Dreamland Auditorium on December 4, 1931.

Canto also wanted another shot at Midget Wolgast. Tom Donahue arranged a rematch, a 10-round bout in San Francisco's Dreamland Auditorium on December 11, 1931. Canto fought very well up to the fifth round, confusing Wolgast with relentless, pounding aggressiveness. Canto was landing his blows with pinpoint accuracy and had a slight lead going into the fifth, but then Canto broke his right hand again, and the bout had to be stopped in the fifth round.

Again, Canto had to take time off to heal and rest. And again, this time away from the rigors of his usual training regimen hurt Canto in his return to the ring. Canto fought Young Tommy in the Dreamland Auditorium in San Francisco on February 2, 1932, lost the match, and fought a rematch one month later, which Canto also lost. Canto fought both of these bouts with a still-broken right hand and with blurred vision.

Canto needed another win to put him back on a winning streak. One month after his second loss to Young Tommy, Canto battled

Benny Gallup in Stockton, California and won by a knockout in the seventh round. The following month, Canto traveled to Seattle, Washington, to take on Ros Dumaguilas and won the match in a six-round decision.

On July 27, 1932 Canto fought the mighty Speedy Dado in Seattle, Washington. This fight resulted in another controversial draw. Seven days later, again in Seattle, Canto fought Dado again and lost in a split decision. Speedy Dado and Canto's rivalry would result in five matches total, with three draws and one win apiece. This rivalry was one of the best-known and admired in Canto's career.

As the second half of 1932 marched forward, Canto continued pursuing opponents and adding victories to his resume. In August 26, also in Seattle, Canto fought a tough upcoming prospect by the name of Rodolfo Teglia and earned himself a draw.

And then fate intervened: Canto fought his last professional bout on September 7, 1932. It was a 6-round match in Seattle against Hilo Hernandez. Canto won in a unanimous decision.

In a career spanning three-and-one-half years, Canto had fought 42 professional fights, with an impressive record overall of 27 wins, 10 draws, and 5 losses, with a total of 13 knockouts. Canto, at age 20, was still young, with the world watching and a lifetime ahead of him. But his life's dream of being a world champion came to a crashing halt.

CHAPTER 6:
Blood on the Canvas

৬৯৬

September 7, 1932,
Bristol Apartments, Seattle, Washington
10 A.M.

Canto and Concha moved to Seattle, Washington in 1931 because Canto was having regular matches in that city. He had already fought six fights in Seattle prior to the upcoming fight with Hilo Hernandez. Canto's training and conditioning took place in Seattle with his manager Tom Donahue, who also moved to the city. Canto and Concha lived in a rented apartment and visited their family back home by train as often as they could.

On September 7, as sunlight gleamed through the stained-glass window, Canto lay in bed relaxing, thinking about his upcoming fight with Hilo Hernandez. He cuddled with his beloved Concha, his guiding force throughout the ups and downs of his career and the pain he had endured through injuries in the ring. She hugged him tightly as she lay in his arms and whispered, "I love you, Canto." Young, beautiful, and petite with black wavy hair, she smiled with deep affection into her husband's eyes. The newlyweds were blissfully serene.

Canto felt reflective. He told his wife: "We are so fortunate and blessed in this horrible Depression. So many people out there searching for food in garbage cans, standing in bread and soup lines, just for something to eat." He held his wife closely and sighed. "So I'm very grateful for everything we have, for this money I'm making tonight."

The $500 purse was more money than most people with jobs were able to earn in a year's time. Canto and Concha knew this well. This Great Depression, the worst economic disaster to hit our country, was a time when banks were closing and people in some places were committing suicide. Despite the dangers of serious injury in the boxing ring, or the dangers of injury during Canto's rigorous training regimen, the couple knew that, through Canto, the Robledo family was lucky to have good money for their needs. He feels this fight will be a blessing for him tonight.

The lovebirds were lost in thought on this momentous day, waiting for the hour in which Canto had to once again prove to the world that he was a champion. They hugged each other more tightly. Suddenly there was a knock on the door, and a voice called out to Canto, "It's time for the weigh-in."

Canto's manager, Tom Donahue, and his trainer Otto walked in. Donahue was a tall, lean, well-dressed middle-aged man with red hair and broad, muscular shoulders. He wore wire-rimmed glasses, and his wrinkled face sometimes looked harsh. This day, he appeared more nervous than usual, and he brusquely told Canto, "Hurry so we won't be late for the weigh-in. Let's get going."

Concha gave Canto a tight hug and a sweet kiss on his cheek. The manager and trainer rushed her husband out the door and into the street where a taxi awaited them.

Otto turned to Canto and reassured him, sensing his nervousness. "You're the best bantamweight fighter in the business," he said. "If you win this fight tonight, you'll get a rematch main event fight with Midget Wolgast."

Canto nodded and smiled at him.

"Stay focused and keep your cool, Canto, because this Hilo Hernandez is a mean son of a bitch who likes to torment his opponents," said Otto. "He likes to swear and will say derogatory things about you and your family. He's a cocky ass who will try to intimidate you into a pushing and shouting match. Hilo wants you to lose your cool. You gotta ignore his trash-talking and remain calm."

Canto listened closely to his trainer's advice, as he'd long ago learned to do. Canto understood the importance of tonight's fight.

He replied to Otto, "It'll be okay. I'll just let him sound off. I won't allow him to distract me." He smiled and shrugged. "After all, I am the Bantamweight Champion of the Pacific Coast."

In boxing, the weigh-in is considered an important aspect of the fight game. This is where the public gets to see the physical shape of the boxer's body, his muscle tone, how lean and trim his body looks, and how strong his arms and legs appear. Does he have a flat nose? Is there any scar tissue above the eyes? And, of course, what is his final weight for the night's fight?

৵৵

The weigh-in at the Civic Ice Arena in Seattle was scheduled for 11:00 AM. Both fighters arrived on time and were anxious and ready for the press to ask questions. A state athletic boxing inspector greeted Canto and said to him and his team, "How's it going, champ? Good luck tonight."

They eventually arrived in their dressing room and were quickly ushered into a large space filled with boxing inspectors and a medical doctor. Sports writers were also present. As the fighters sat at the table, they were peppered with questions. The camera bulbs flashed and reporters rushed to the interview table anxious for close-up pictures of both fighters. Canto found himself sitting next to Hilo Hernandez, who was already badgering Canto with trashy words and menacing looks.

"So, you're the tough Mexican kid who thinks one day you will be fighting for the world's title? No way! Not tonight! I'll knock you out early and wipe the canvas with your blood!" said Hilo under his breath to Canto. "You must go through me first. Your boxing career will be over. I'm gonna knock you out cold."

The State of Washington boxing inspector announced to the press: "Canto Robleto, Pasadena, California, weighing in at 118 pounds, and wearing blue trunks, trimmed in white stripes. His record is 25 wins, 11 losses, and 5 draws."

The inspector then announced: "His opponent tonight, fighting out of Hawaii, is Hilo Hernandez, weighing in at 118 pounds, wearing solid black trunks, with a fine record of 11 wins, 5 losses, and one draw."

Canto finished the weigh-in and calmly walked back to the car. Sitting in the back seat, Otto said to Canto, "You have to be careful! Hilo is a strong, rough and tough fighter; he's a world class contender but he's known for his dirty tricks in the ring."

"What do you mean dirty tricks?" asked Canto.

Donahue chimed in: "Hilo likes to thumb fighters with the glove and uses his elbows in the clinches." At this time, boxing gloves included movable, protruding thumbs.

Canto returned to the Bristol Apartments to be with Concha, who had been anxiously waiting for him. She rushed to the door as Canto arrived and greeted him with a kiss and strong embrace. Canto held her tight and kissed her cheek. Concha then prepared Canto's favorite dinner: top sirloin steak, macaroni and cheese with some mixed vegetables, and orange juice. She reflected on how content she was as Canto's wife. She would do anything for him.

After dinner, the couple sat comfortably on a nice leather sofa as they listened to soft, Spanish love songs on the radio. Canto loved Concha with all his heart and soul. They often sang to one another when they relaxed together or lay in bed at night. Tonight, in their peaceful bliss, she asked Canto if he wanted to pray the rosary with her to ask for a good outcome at the fight and for protection from harm. This ritual was a very calming time for Canto, a time of deep meditation and relaxation. He felt peaceful in Concha's presence.

She was seriously concerned with Canto's throbbing headaches, burning and painful eyes, along with complaints of blurry vision. Concha had been encouraging Canto to have his eyes checked and the large bump on his right hand treated medically. She had pleaded with him often to place his boxing career on hold while he gave his body ample time to be fully healed. All this to no avail.

Canto had told her a few times that hard punches to his temple and resin from the boxing apron had combined to damage his eyes. He experienced burning sensations affecting his vision. He cited his signed contract with Tom Donahue as his reason for not taking a leave of absence from boxing. He had no choice, he told her

"But I promise you, after this fight, I will have my eyes and hand checked," he assured her.

❧❧

Canto's dressing room was a large rectangular area with a rubdown table, a shower, a closet for clothes, a small sink, and a clock on the wall. Canto sat on the rubdown table, thinking, *I must win tonight. I have to defeat this tough one from Hawaii. I must protect myself, and my eyes. I feel positive and confident! I've worked and trained hard for this fight. All the personal sacrifices, the early morning runs, the endless sparring, the sweating and the bruises on my body—all these things have prepared me for this fight!*

In Canto's dressing room, his trainers looked at the clock. It was almost time for the fight to begin. The sustained noise of the crowd penetrated the walls of the locker area, along with the drumbeats of their thumping feet. The crowd was large, anxious, and expecting a hell of a good fight. Calm and composed, Canto envisioned the fight ahead.

Otto checked all the boxing equipment, including the mouthpiece, cutting tape, the gauze that would wrap the hands, and ice for the bucket. He washed all the water bottles and filled them with tap water. He looked closely at Canto's mouthpiece, making sure it had no cracks or breaks. The cup was laced and tightened around Canto's waist. His terry cloth robe hung ready in the corner. The back of the robe read *Canto 'TNT' Robleto*.

Canto knew that a win tonight would mean perhaps an eventual title fight with Panama Al Brown. Many other thoughts raced through his mind. He badly wanted to become a world champion. He would be the first in his family to achieve this goal. Canto would be able to buy a home for his wife and for his parents.

❧❧

Canto was favored to win. He sat with Tom Donahue and Otto in the dressing room, preparing for the fight with Hilo Hernandez. Canto was the darling of the Pacific Coast, and the reporters loved him. They predicted an early knockout for him. His manager ignored the questions from reporters and ordered the press to leave or else he would call security to have them removed from the dressing area.

Canto was ready to leave the dressing room now and enter the boxing ring, or "square circle," as it's called in the sport. His hand wraps were ready, gloves laced up, mouthpiece in place, cup secured, and trunks and shoes were on. The robe was draped over Canto's shoulders. First, though, he wanted to say a final prayer. He knelt on the cold concrete floor and prayed from the bottom of his heart.

Canto, manager, and trainer walked out of the dressing room to the beat of chants loud and rhythmic: *Canto! Canto! Canto!* The walk to the ring was nerve-wracking. Canto was full of anticipation and the so-called butterflies. He walked up the steps and climbed onto the ring's canvas, jumping over the top strand of ropes, a trademark of Canto "TNT" Robleto.

In the ring, he began to shadow box, throwing a flurry of punches. The crowd went wild for him. As Canto looked across the ring, he noticed his opponent staring and glaring at him, as if to say, "I'm going to knock you out tonight! The Pacific Bantamweight title will be mine!" Canto reassured himself: *I will win tonight at any price.*

The fighters and corner men were instructed to clear the ring and prepare for the fight. Each fighter was now ready, their eyebrows and noses gleaming with the light layers of Vaseline their trainers smeared on their faces to make gloves slide off the face rather than cut.

The ring announcer lifted his megaphone and began his spiel to introduce the fighters.

"Welcome, ladies and gentlemen, to the main event of the evening. In the red corner from the great state of Hawaii, weighing in at 118 pounds, with a fine ring record of 11 wins, 5 losses, and one draw, wearing black trunks trimmed in white, please welcome the heavy hitter, Hilo Hernandez!"

The crowd roared, cheered, and screamed with anticipation for Hilo. The young fighter raised his hand high in the air and bowed to the crowd.

The announcer then turned to Canto: "In the blue corner from Pasadena, California, weighing in at a trim 118 pounds, with an outstanding record of 26 wins, 10 losses, and 5 draws, 9 wins by knockout, wearing blue trunks trimmed in white stripes, please welcome the Pacific Coast Bantamweight Champion, Canto TNT Robleto!"

The crowd went wild, and Canto's heart thumped with excitement and gratitude for his fans. Both fighters met in the center of the ring, where the referee intoned the standard rules: "Keep your punches above the waist, no rabbit punches (boxing term for hitting behind the head). Let's have a clean fight. Now, touch gloves!"

Both fighters returned to their respective corners. Canto genuflected and crossed himself, his lips moving in a brief prayer. *This is it! I must win!* he thought to himself. He began bouncing on his toes and waited for the bell to sound.

❧❧

Bristol Apartments, Seattle Washington,
8:00 P.M.

Concha, and her friend Frances sat on the sofa in the front room of Concha's apartment. They were listening intently to the radio. Just then the announcer said: "Welcome, ladies and gentlemen, to the main event of the evening…."

This was the broadcast of Canto's fight. The women heard the crowd's roars and chanting: CANTO! CANTO! CANTO! Concha's eyes filled with tears, a combination of pride in her husband's popularity and pride that she was his wife.

Frances asked her, "Why didn't you go to the arena? It would've been so exciting to be there rooting for Canto!"

Concha shook her head. "He didn't want me to go, not tonight. He had this strange feeling for a few days. He insisted I stay home."

The women, consigned now to only what the radio hosts would be reporting, settled more comfortably into the sofa and leaned toward the radio. Despite being across town, the women felt like they were there at ringside, with Canto, amidst the boxers' blows, the fans' cheers, and the agitated descriptions of the radio commentators.

When Hilo Hernandez threw the punch that cut Canto's right eye on the eyebrow, and his blood dripped onto the canvas, Concha felt as if she herself had been punched in the gut. Then, when Canto mistakenly punched the referee, Concha cringed. The crowd booed when Canto, confused and unable to see clearly, mistook the referee for Hilo and struck the referee, sending him to the canvas. The referee, stunned and angry, warned Canto not to do this again to him, or Canto would be disqualified. Canto was shocked at his mistake.

61

Blow by blow, Concha endured what she knew was the progression of her husband's damaged eyesight, and the immense pain he was suffering, and her heart was torn.

In the arena, the crowd was as wild in the middle of the fight as they'd been at the beginning. Canto had been hit powerfully in the face again and again by Hilo Hernandez and bled profusely while seated in his corner, getting wiped and attended to by his worried trainer. The crowd saw Otto and Donahue arguing in their corner between rounds, but they didn't know the two men were debating whether or not the fight should be stopped to save Canto's eyesight.

As the fight continued, Canto absorbed more and more vicious punches to his eyes, along with Hilo's dirty tricks with his elbows and thumbs in Canto's eyes as often as the Hawaiian could get these pokes in. Eventually Canto's vision faded almost completely. But soon after the punching of the referee, Canto pulled himself together, summoned the intense willpower of a champ, and landed enough blows on Hilo to regain the early lead he'd built in the fight.

The final bell clanged. The fight was over, and Canto won a split decision. He, Donahue, and Otto left the ring quickly and rushed to the dressing room, as Canto demanded. Canto also kept his gloves on at the end of the fight because he could no longer see and would be unable to sign autographs.

"Hurry! Get me to the dressing room!" Canto said through gritted teeth immediately after the fight ended. "Hold my arm. I'm seeing spots and sparks. Everything's getting darker. Don't let the press near me! Get me back to the locker room!"

Away from the crowds, Canto lay confused and concerned on the rubdown table, while Otto and Tom Donahue tried to reassure him. The three men, alone in the dressing room now, away from the press and fans, realized that Canto's eye injuries were so severe, he had most likely lost his vision. Otto had tried to stop the fight, but Tom Donahue, the manager, had insisted that Canto continue.

As Canto lay on the table, Donahue said: "I called the ophthalmologist, and he wants us to bring you over to his office immediately. Because of the severity of the situation, he's willing to make a trip to his office to examine you right away."

Could this be the final bout and a tragic end of the highly successful fighting career of Canto "TNT" Robleto, Pacific Coast Bantamweight Champion?

CHAPTER 7:
A Future Hopeless and Unsure

Donahue and Otto took Canto directly from his dressing room to the eye doctor they had alerted. During the drive to the ophthalmologist's office, Canto felt sure that he would not be able to regain his eyesight. He regretted not having listened to his wife, and regretted taking the Hilo Hernandez fight as well.

The doctor was waiting for them. He examined Canto's eyes and immediately saw that the injuries were extensive to both eyes. The doctor put all sorts of drops into Canto's eyes, hoping to relieve the burning and pressure from them, and covered Canto's right eye as a precaution against further damage. When he finished his examination, he told Canto that his fighting days were over.

"I suggest you hang up the gloves unless you want to go blind!" the doctor intoned.

The doctor described in medical terms what was wrong with the eyes. Fearful and frustrated with the doctor's mumbo-jumbo, Canto interrupted him and blurted, "Doc, give it to me straight so I can understand! What the hell is wrong with my eyes?"

"Canto, I suspect there is serious damage to both eyes, though the right eye has suffered the most. We need to do further testing to confirm this. At best, you'll need to have eye surgery to try to repair the damaged retina. Unfortunately, I have little experience in the field of repairing torn or detached retinas."

Canto was incredulous. How could this be happening to him? He sat stunned on the examining table and had to be led by his manager and trainer to his car. The drive back to Canto's apartment seemed endless as he rehashed the doctor's words over and over again. He asked himself, *Now what am I going to tell my wife and my family?* Canto was in a state of shock. *How am I going to make a living? What the hell am I going to do now with failing eyes?*

❧❧

Returning Home

Canto and Concha's train ride from Seattle to Los Angeles was a long, sad ride with many unanswered questions. The only comfort to Canto was having his beloved wife by his side. At this point he had little vision remaining in his left eye, and the vision in the right eye was worse: darkness, murkiness, not even shadows or light. How quickly his fighting career was over!

Canto's father Felipe and mother Soledad met Canto and Concha at the train station and immediately drove home to avoid the press, who were waiting to get an interview with Canto. Many children of Mexican descent were playing and waiting for Canto in the family's front yard. Uncles, aunts, and cousins were milling about, anxiously waiting for Canto and Concha's return home from Seattle. Many concerned and admiring people wanted to greet them and welcome them home.

But Canto was not in a mood to talk with anyone because of the pain in his eyes and his tumultuous state of mind. He was rushed quickly into the back door to avoid everyone and was guided by his father into one of the bedrooms, where he tripped, then regained his balance quickly and sat down on the bed. It was close to dinnertime, and food was being prepared for him and Concha.

"I'm not hungry. I don't want to eat," he said sadly.

Inside the house, his siblings looked out the front window and wondered what they could say to the concerned, excited gathering of extended family members and assorted friends still waiting on the lawn to see Canto. Canto's older brother Benny eventually went outside to talk to everyone, but he wasn't quite sure what to tell them about Canto's condition other than Canto was having problems with his eyesight.

It was a sad homecoming. Canto had been victorious in his match. These people gathered outside were not only family, but also neighbors and friends. They were fans who were proud of him, the "native son" of Pasadena who had made them feel proud with his boxing accomplishments. A cloud of uncertainty and sadness descended mercilessly upon them.

Canto and Concha moved in with his parents on 687 Cypress Street so they could help care for Canto. Concha was 18 years old, still a newlywed, and pregnant with their first child. A resourceful young woman fully devoted to her husband, she quickly became part of the Robledo family, as if she had been born a Robledo. During the time she and Canto had lived in Seattle for the sake of his career, she had missed Pasadena, her beloved city. She was happy to be back home, though now "home" was not their own apartment.

Concha's family still lived in East Pasadena on Linda Rosa Court, and now she was able to visit her parents and her siblings more often than when she'd lived far away. Returning to Pasadena after Canto's injury and facing his pain each day was a tough journey for the young couple. Concha recounted this journey to her family, and they were concerned for him. The Jimenez family had always been close-knit, and they embraced Canto as their son and wanted to do whatever they could for him and Concha in their difficult situation.

Amidst the sadness of Canto's loss of vision, pain, and despair, Concha took solace in her pregnancy. Expecting her first child was a supreme joy to her, and she wanted it to be for Canto as well. Her family accepted that she had to live in the Canto family home to tend to her husband. Their baby was due in January, just four months away. So much was happening in Concha's young life, but she knew having her family and the Robledo family around both her and Canto would make their lives easier, and she was hopeful about their future.

A Visit with the Eye Doctor

In the office of the eye specialist, Dr. Grove, in downtown Los Angeles, Canto waited anxiously with Concha and his father at his side. The doctor entered the examination room and greeted them warmly, assuring Canto that he'd do everything he could for him.

"Hopefully we can help you regain your vision in both eyes," the doctor said.

He removed the protective patch from Canto's right eye and placed various drops in both eyes. He then asked Canto to read the letters on the eye chart. Canto was unable to make out any letters. He told the doctor that he could see nothing at all from his right eye and the left eye was just slightly better.

The doctor then had Canto put his chin on the ledge of his large eye exam machine, a phoroptor, and began flipping dials and lenses up and down, asking Canto to move his eyes up, down, and sideways. Dr. Grove looked through his various instruments to check Canto's retinas. He could see that the retina in the right eye was detached and the retina in the left eye was partially torn. His visual acuity was blurred in the left eye and there was no vision in the right eye, which had sustained the full force of the first blow to Canto's eyes in his last boxing match.

The doctor gave Canto the bad news: "We have little experience in repairing detached retinas, and there is no chance of an eye transplant."

Seeing Canto's disappointment and his family's sadness, the doctor tried to give them some hope.

"In a few years," he said in measured tones, "we may have more knowledge about eye transplants and repairing detached retinas. We'll have to wait and see what the future brings."

The family was devastated. On their return trip home, their grief was almost palpable. At home, Canto sat quietly in his room, a gloom filling the air. The shades on the window had been drawn shut. Concha sat with him, trying to talk to him, but there was little conversation between the two of them. She reached for his hand and held it tightly, but Canto pulled his hand away and shook his head in despair.

"Leave me while you're still young and beautiful," he said to her softly. "You'll be able to find someone to take care of you and give you a good family life."

His face was firm and his eyes were turned away from her.

"Look at me," he said, turning toward her. "I'm almost all blind now. Soon I may be. I don't have any way of providing for you. We have a baby on the way. How can I support you both? Please, go. Leave me while you can."

It broke his heart to say this and broke her heart to hear it. Her baby bump was beginning to show. She felt so proud to be carrying his child. She shook her head and held him closely, murmuring her assurances that she'd never leave him.

"Think of how happy we'll be when the baby comes," she said.

*ઠ*ઠ

For days, Canto sat all alone in his darkened bedroom contemplating the past and the future. The future for him looked incredibly bleak and offered no possibility of work. He pondered life without working to support himself, without being able to support his young family. *If I can't see to work*, he said to himself, *then there will be no work, no hope.*

Canto's mother walked into the bedroom, closing the door softly behind her. There was a strong family resemblance between Canto and his mother. Soledad's face was sad, worn, and full of anguish, but she was always a woman of strong faith in the Lord and hoping for a miracle for her son. Sitting on the bed next to her son, she tried to break through his self-imposed isolation.

"Everything will be fine, Canto," she said calmly. "Have faith."

He didn't respond.

"I want you to go with me to visit the Virgin Mary," she said to him. Her family regularly visited a well-known shrine in Sunland, a city in Southern California about half an hour away from Pasadena.

"No," Canto replied angrily.

"Your father is going to drive the family," said Soledad.

"Mother, how many times have I told you? I'm not going."

Undeterred, Soledad remained calm. "Miracles happen all the time, Canto. Don't you believe in miracles?"

He stayed silent.

"Don't you believe in God?" she asked him.

He replied softly. "Yes, but not for damaged eyes that have been ruined like mine have been."

His words tugged at her heart. She embraced him.

"You are my son, and we are a family of faith," she replied softly. "I love you and will always love you, and you must have faith in the Almighty Lord."

"What faith, Mother?" he said sharply. "Faith didn't protect me. I prayed before the fight. I knelt and made the sign of the cross right there in the ring. Concha and I prayed before I went to the ring. What good did all this do for me?"

His voice was angry but tired and anxious.

"All my faith didn't protect me. It left me in darkness," he continued. He seemed resigned and out of energy.

Soledad took Canto's hand and held it tightly, not wanting to let go.

"Please go with us, my son."

He was scared and began to weep in his mother's arms. He knew the depth of his mother's faith and how hard she had worked in their home to give him a good life, how hard she had supported all his dreams.

He finally stopped weeping and said quietly, "OK, for you I will go."

His mother was relieved and happy that he'd be going to the Shrine of the Virgin Mary. She held Canto tightly and kissed him on the cheek. For the first time since coming home, Canto smiled.

෴

It was a bright sunny morning when the Robledos made their journey to Sunland to visit the site of the Shrine of the Blessed Virgin Mary, the mother of Jesus Christ. Many of Canto's Catholic friends knew about the shrine and, like Soledad, had wanted Canto to visit this holy place.

The Virgin Mary statue was in an antiquated, wood-framed cabin, the shrine, that was solidly built. This small house was unpainted and fading. It sat in the backyard of a front house on a deep lot. Avocado and shade trees dotted the landscape. Underneath the trees were wooden chairs, where people would stop and rest, many of the people having walked for miles to come and pray. The statue of the Virgin Mary was ensconced in the wooden structure, surrounded by many spiritual and primitive artifacts. The single room of the structure had a few movable cushion kneelers for praying. Several chairs lined the walls for sitting, meditating, and praying. The old wooden floor creaked with the pilgrims' footsteps as they moved about the room. A very soft light came from the clusters of candles that surrounded the Virgin Mary. The statue stood inside a large glass case, which was surrounded by many fresh flowers brought every day by the countless visitors to this holy place.

Canto was led to the shrine by Concha. She held his hand tightly, guiding him into the wooden house in the back lot and inside this shrine up to the encased Virgin Mary statue. Canto asked where the statue was, and Concha tenderly tilted his face slightly upward as if to be looking into the statue's eyes. Concha whispered to him, "She is looking down on you now."

Canto looked up, then knelt on a soft cushion on the floor before the Virgin. As he did so, a sense of peace and serenity overcame him. Canto beseeched the Blessed Mother Mary for her intercession for a miracle of healing of both eyes. He felt that this holy place could make his prayers come true. In the rear of the room, Canto's parents knelt piously in prayer. Suddenly, Canto turned his head as he heard something in the room.

"Is there a faint singing somewhere?" he asked Concha. He wondered if angels were singing to him.

Without warning, he felt a terrible, burning pain in his right eye. He leaned forward, moaning, groaning, and pressed his hand over the eye.

"It's like a heart in my eye is bleeding," said Canto, "and a sharp knife is penetrating the eye. A white light. It looks like a white light is coming into the eye."

Concha held him as he spoke. "It could be a sign, Canto," she said to him. "Perhaps a miracle is happening."

⋖ઝ⋗

The Great Depression made life much more difficult, not only for the Robledo and Jimenez families, but for everyone. The economy continued to decline, and unemployment increased to 24.1 percent.

There were few jobs, with countless ordinary Americans forced into living in the streets or in old cars. Many people got their food in soup and bread lines. American voters disgusted with President Herbert Hoover used the power of democracy to oust him from power and voted strongly in favor of Franklin D. Roosevelt by a landslide.

The Emergency Relief and Construction Act was enacted, one of many changes to bring relief to people's suffering. This was the United States' first major relief legislation to fund the public works administration (WPA), hoping to put millions of Americans back to work, initiated by Herbert Hoover and later adopted and expanded by Roosevelt as part of "The New Deal." Drought conditions and over-mechanization of farming caused great areas of the Midwest to become dustbowls, another major blow to the economy. So the nation's fortunes, some up, some down, reflected the turmoil Canto and his family found themselves in.

Three months after their visit to the Shrine, Canto and Concha sat on the patio. Things hadn't changed much for them: Canto was still unemployed, and the days dragged by.

"You just can't sit here day after day and waste your life away," Concha said to him.

"It doesn't matter anymore," said Canto flatly. "Everything is gone. Every doctor wants to try something new. But there is no relief from the pain, and I still have no vision."

Concha's soul felt his frustration. "There are other specialists we can find."

Canto turned his face towards her voice. "Where are we going to get that kind of money for a specialist?"

"Canto, we can't give up hope. So many people are praying for you," replied Concha.

With a deep frustration, Canto asked: "Where in the hell is my manager, Tom Donahue? Where is the money he owes me? He promised he would be there for me."

The memory of Donahue refusing to stop Canto's fight with Hilo Hernandez was still clear in Canto's mind.

"That bum has run off with the money he owes me!" said Canto.

Please Come and Eat, Canto

As the days and weeks passed, Canto refused more and more often to come out of his room and eat in the kitchen with his family. He was in a deep state of depression and was beginning to hear voices. His eyes continued to burn with excruciating pain. His headaches were painful, throbbing, constant, and he had suicidal thoughts.

One day, Concha walked into their darkened bedroom and found Canto in a fetal position, huddled in the closet. She had brought Canto some food, since he hadn't eaten for days. Her pregnancy was now advanced. She begged him to come out and spend some time visiting with the aunts, uncles, and cousins who came daily to see him and talk some hope into him. But Canto refused.

Concha, deeply concerned, said to him: "There's no reason to lock yourself up in a closet."

His behavior was increasingly alarming to her and the rest of the family.

"Leave me alone," said Canto. "I don't want you to stay with me any longer. Please leave me alone. I'll fight my own battles."

Concha left, closing the door softly behind her. Canto hungrily ate the food she'd brought him. He wanted to listen to her, to believe her words, but he was in his own world of sadness, his faith fading fast. His chest tightened and heaved with sobs, then he began to weep long and deeply until he cried himself to sleep.

Later, Canto would recount the dream he had to his family:

For the first time since his injury in the ring, Canto was able to physically see something clearly in his dream. He saw scenes of good times he was having with Concha in his daily life with her. He saw them dancing and taking walks on the beach as they'd done before the fight. He saw Concha's loveliness, which had made him fall in love with her the first time he saw her. He saw the tall Sequoias, redwoods, and the beautiful shoreline of the Pacific Coast.

In this dream, Canto saw a possibility of a miracle. He felt the spirit of God and a renewed determination to live. He wanted to stay with Concha and be a family, if Concha was willing to forgive him and move forward with him.

In this dream, someone was going to come to him and help him, someone with special skills and talent. This was a little seed of hope germinating in his spirit.

But when he awakened from this dream, Canto's depression felt overpowering and, once again, he plunged into a state of sadness.

CHAPTER 8:
The Darkness Deepens

Dr. Walker was a tall, sharp, middle-aged man with a kind, thoughtful face. He was out here in Los Angeles from Virginia for a series of Anatomical and Physiological lectures at Good Samaritan Hospital, since he was a leading specialist in the field of detached retinas and ophthalmology.

Dr. Walker was in the lecture hall, putting his lecture notes and textbook away, when the door opened quietly, and a beautiful, gentle Mexican woman with long brown hair approached him. Without introductions or other preface, the woman begged him to go see Canto Robledo, a 20-year-old Mexican boy who had lost his eyesight in the boxing ring. He is married, the angelic woman said, and his wife is pregnant. He is almost completely blind. She urged the doctor to intervene.

"Canto is here now at the hospital," she said. "Can you please take a moment to see if there's anything you can do to help him?"

An inexplicable feeling of urgency overcame the doctor, compelling him to take this case. Dr. Walker used the hospital phone to call his nurse to see if she had any information or a medical file on someone named Canto Robledo. If so, could she please bring the files to him in the examination room. He also instructed her to bring patient Canto Robledo as well.

In the examination room, Canto sat quietly with Concha at his side. The doctor walked in, introduced himself, and told them of his encounter with the beautiful Mexican woman. The doctor described to the couple how this woman had informed him about Canto, that he was 20 years old, almost totally blind, married, with a pregnant wife, and how this woman had pleaded with the doctor to see Canto. The doctor asked Canto who this woman was. Canto and Concha were surprised. They didn't know anyone who had done this.

Canto replied, "I don't know, doctor, but I had a dream that the Virgin Mary was going to send a doctor to help me."

The doctor didn't know how to reply, so he explained to Canto that he would examine him, but first he had to dilate the eyes and wait fifteen minutes before the eyes could be checked. Canto was apprehensive and hopeful at the same time. At this point in time, he believed the Virgin Mary had sent this doctor to restore his vision. The eye specialist began the exam by looking into Canto's right eye with an ophthalmoscope.

"Do you see any light?"

"No," said Canto.

The doctor was able to see the retina and could see it was completely detached. He mentioned nothing of this to Canto but began examining the left eye. The doctor saw that the retina was partially torn.

"Canto, can you read the letters on the chart on the wall?"

"What letters, doctor?" asked Canto.

"On the chart," said the doctor again.

"I can't see any letters," said Canto.

The doctor realized that this was a very serious injury to both eyes. "What happened to your eyes, Canto?"

"My last fight was a rough fight. My opponent kept thumbing me in the eyes, and sometimes even elbowing me in the face and eyes, especially my right eye. That's when my vision left me."

Dr. Walker informed Canto and Concha the state of damage he found in both eyes. Cautiously optimistic, he said: "There is a slight chance I may be able to repair the retina in the left eye, but I can't give you any guarantees. An operation of this nature is extremely difficult and has inherent dangers. Your right eye, though, is completely beyond repair. Maybe in a couple years we'll have more advanced knowledge about retina repairs."

Concha broke down and started to cry. Canto held her in his arms. "We have to stay strong for the family," he said. "It'll be okay. We'll make the best of it."

After the eye examination, Canto and Concha were escorted to the waiting room and instructed not to leave the hospital. The doctor had told them he would perform the surgery immediately.

Surgery with Dr. Walker

In a bright room at the Los Angeles County Hospital, an assistant surgeon and a surgical nurse prepared for the operation.

"Is Dr. Clifton Walker really performing this operation?" asked the assistant surgeon. "It sounds like a celebrity case."

"No," replied nurse Goldberg, "just a Mexican, a charity case."

"What do you mean?"

"Dr. Walker was out here from Virginia for a series of lectures, when the doctor was approached by a Mexican lady who pleaded and begged with him to look into the case."

The door opened, and Dr. Walker entered the room. He greeted his surgical team.

"Dr. Walker, Nurse Goldberg was telling me about this unusual case."

"Yes, very unusual circumstances indeed, a kind of a miracle if you believe in that sort of thing."

Dr. Walker began his cleansing preparations with Nurse Goldberg's assistance.

"So whatever happened to that Mexican lady who begged you to take this case?" asked the nurse.

"She simply vanished," said the doctor casually as he shrugged his shoulders. "I'm not really sure she was ever there, actually. She said something about him being a boxer and that seemed to fit the eye problem she said he had."

Dr. Walker instructed the nurse to bring Canto Robledo in. She walked into the waiting room and asked Canto to follow her. He stood on his own two feet and with confidence made his way past the family members who had gathered in solidarity and went with the nurse, who was now holding his arm to guide him. Dr. Walker was in the surgery room preparing his surgical instruments.

"Is it possible you can restore any vision?" asked the assistant surgeon when he saw Canto being guided in.

"Prognosis hopeless. I haven't prayed for years, but I did just now," said the doctor.

The nurse guided him to the surgical bed. The anesthesiologist brought in his equipment, Canto listening all the while with his acute hearing, trying to sense the environment.

Dr. Walker asked Canto, "Can you see anything out of your right eye?"

"No, doctor."

"How about the left eye?"

"Just a little light but not clear. Everything seems fuzzy and blurry."

"Canto, after I conduct the procedure, I'll ask you if you see anything."

Canto replied, "I'm scared, doctor, more than ever."

"I understand, but just like in the ring, you've got to stay tough, strong, and have faith."

The nurse placed the equipment next to the bed.

"Nurse, hold his head, and turn it towards the light," the doctor said. "Canto, we're about to administer the pain medication. We need you to stay conscious as I proceed."

"Pain is nothing new to me, doctor. I'll do whatever it takes to get my eyesight back." Canto took a deep breath. "I trust you. I believe you'll do everything you can for me."

"Relax as much as possible, focus on your loving wife, think of the happy times you have had with her," the doctor advised.

Canto closed his eyes and reflected briefly on the love he and Concha had for one another and all that lay ahead for them. He tried not to cry.

"Nurse, sponge the right temple toward the eyelid. Hold his head steady."

Dr. Walker held up his hands, staring, maybe praying. He moved in closely with his surgical stool. The nurse was ready with a syringe with a morphine solution. Dr. Walker slowly adjusted the direct light and picked up a slender scalpel.

"Canto, I'm going to make an incision into the eyeball."

The light stream of blood that flowed was instantly wiped away by a small suction funnel in the hand of the nurse. Canto, unable to relax, held tensely onto the edges of his bed. Dr. Walker ordered that he be given the shot of morphine to calm him.

The surgery was soon over. Canto was taken to a recovery ward and left alone while being restrained to the bed. Dr. Walker went to the waiting room to notify Concha and the other family members waiting with her that the surgery had gone well, without any complications. He added that Canto would need to remain hospitalized for observation and much-needed rest.

"It's too early for me to tell if he'll be able to see again," he told them. "We'll just have to wait and see."

For the next day or two, Canto drifted in and out of consciousness. When he awakened, he struggled against the arm restraints that had been added to the bed for his safety. He became agitated and began yelling for the nurse. No one responded, and he felt lonely without Concha and his family. Unbeknownst to him, they were waiting just outside the recovery ward and were able to hear him calling out for help.

They scurried to the ward and saw him struggling with the protective arm restraints. The loud moaning, groaning and crying of another patient was upsetting Canto. The family became unsettled with what they considered an awful atmosphere in the room, and they demanded that Canto be moved to a quieter, calmer ward. The hospital denied their request due to hospital rules and regulations.

After the family left, Canto's situation in the loud ward worsened. The orderly on duty, a broad-shouldered, impatient man, snapped angrily at Canto when he asked for anything.

"Shut up!" the crude orderly said to Canto at one point. "I'll attend to you when I get to you." When he walked by Canto's bed, the orderly jabbed Canto on the side of the body and walked away as if nothing had happened.

Canto settled down on the bed when he discovered a tiny beam of light entering from the tip of the protective cone around his eye. The light was dim at first but seemed to be getting brighter. Canto yelled out with joy and excitement and struggled again to be free of the restraints. The orderly tightened the straps firmly and told Canto again, "Shut the hell up!"

Canto was desperate and scared to death. He twisted and turned in bed until he was able to free himself from the restraints. He tried to get out of bed, but he was unceremoniously pushed back onto the bed. He demanded to be let go, but the first orderly was now joined by another one, equally rude and impatient. One of them tried to sock Canto, but Canto knocked him down quickly. The second orderly jumped onto Canto on the bed, while the first orderly scrambled to his feet and socked Canto in the face. The protective cone on Canto's eye was twisted from its careful placement, and Canto's slight field of vision blurred out. Darkness returned instantly with burning pain. Roughed up, Canto was forced back into his bed and secured tightly with double restraints. One orderly gave him a shot of morphine, and Canto blacked out. Days later, Canto returned home.

At home, Canto isolated himself in a cramped, dark closet. He repeated nonsensical words like an incantation. He talked to himself and answered himself. He went for days without a shower, and his hair was dirty and unkempt. He was unshaven and his face bristled with a growing beard. Canto was in deep despair, all hope gone. He heard nonexistent voices, and this bothered him. All he wanted was to be left alone, but Concha would not abandon him or give up on him. Daily, she brought him food and water, encouraging him to eat. Daily, he told her to leave him, then he'd return to the cramped closet again.

But once alone again, hidden out of view of others in the closet, Canto would indeed eat and drink. He'd grab hungrily at the plate and cup and gulp down whatever Concha had brought to him. So in this way, he survived. Sometimes he ate so fast, that he choked and struggled to breathe again. He slid the dishes back out of the closet and wept until he'd fall asleep.

෯෯

Concha delivered a healthy baby girl, whom she named Gloria Virginia, at the Women's Hospital in Pasadena. She was the first grandchild of the Robledo clan. This was a joyful time for the Robledo and Jimenez families, except for Canto. The families welcomed the baby and every moment with her. Gloria was truly a blessing from heaven, yet this was a time that Canto was lost and confused. He now drank heavily and was becoming more disconnected from all he valued. He was unable to accept the fact that he was totally blind in both eyes.

His wife and mother were right at his side. They never gave up hope on Canto. The entire family wanted him to get better, but this was Canto's battle, and no one could help get his eyesight back. He had continued isolating himself in his gloomy room and hardly emerged for more than two months. He occasionally came out to wash up, eat, and chat briefly with Concha.

As time passed, Canto stopped shutting himself away in the closet. He spent more time out of the room and even began relaxing on a cushioned chair in the bedroom, thinking about the past. Once, he stood up and tried to make his way around the bedroom, when he bumped into furniture and nearly fell. He felt his way to the bed and lay on it. He reminisced about his life a mere year ago, when he'd had his sight, was newly married, and was Pacific Coast Bantamweight Champion. All had been going smoothly in his life. What had happened to turn the tide of events so suddenly and tragically?

Canto's mother walked into the bedroom. "Concha will be bringing baby Gloria in to see you," she said.

Canto wasn't happy to hear this. He didn't want to meet the new baby. He bowed his head and folded his hands as if in prayer. Then he cried out, "Why? I can't *see* the baby!"

Just then, Concha entered the bedroom and walked over to Canto. She carefully placed baby Gloria in his arms and said to Canto, "Kiss her and tell her how much you love her."

Canto felt the baby with his hands, her warmth and softness, and smelled the clean, unique smell of babies. He heard her with his sensitive hearing. He held her gently in his arms and suddenly felt a deep love for the child and began to cry. Concha was pleased and happy that Canto was showing these emotions, showing his joy for the baby for the first time. Concha and Canto's mother beamed with pride and gratitude, breaking the gloom of the past months. Canto finally appeared to be making progress.

Canto's body began to shake, and he felt unsteady.

"But I can't *see* her!"

Still shaking, he gave the baby back to Concha and angrily stumbled to the window, ripping the shade violently from its anchor on the wall.

"You have to have faith, Canto." Concha spoke in a calm, soothing voice.

"I had faith once," he retorted.

"Yes, that's right," Concha said. "Your faith in God and the Virgin Mary helped you with that great doctor."

"No! With that doctor, I had my only chance, but everything failed, and now my chance is lost forever! What can God do for me now? Absolutely nothing!"

"Please, Canto, come out of the bedroom, and be with our family. You can't stay here in this room forever!"

"Then I'll go out with my friends!" he said.

"Where would you go, Canto?" Concha asked. She was a bit apprehensive.

"Anywhere, but here. That way you don't have to worry about me, or take care of me!"

"But who would you go with?" she asked in a quivering voice.

"I'll find somebody, anybody that's not in the family! Someone who can take me anywhere from here!"

❧❧

Friday evening found Canto in a low-class, broken-down bar with two bums. Canto was half drunk, and his companions put him on display. One of the bums pointed him out to anyone who would listen and said, "Lookie here. This is Canto Robleto, a boxing champion! Do you want to shake his hand?"

This type of side show bought them drinks, and Canto played his part by shadow boxing and letting go with a series of punches. Often, he would try and fight the man who had been mocking him. He lunged, stumbled, and fell when he attempted this. Someone always picked him up off the floor and put him back on his bar stool.

The bartender yelled at the customers: "Leave him alone! He's blind as a bat now, but at one time he could've been champion of the world."

If people snickered and laughed at this comment, the bartender would calmly say: "He was once the Bantamweight Champion of the Pacific Coast."

Canto continued to spiral out of control with drinking every night. His low-class buddies had become more disrespectful about him, except for his ability to get drinks for them all. They became nastier in their selfish motives in bringing attention to him, and Canto grew more bitter, more angry and destructive in a dangerous way. Canto, both blind and drunk, eventually became vicious in his attacks when taunted. He seemed to beg to be beaten down and smashed into unconsciousness.

Canto, accustomed to feeling despondent with a heavy heart, decided in a sober moment one day that he wanted to visit the Shrine of the Virgin Mary again. He had a deep personal calling and wanted to take a drive to Sunland to visit the shrine. Canto was feeling sorry for himself and needed to find a new way of life. Concha was pleased that Canto was willing to renew his faith in the Lord, trying to turn his life around. This was a big step for Canto.

The Robledo family joined Concha and Canto on the trip. Upon entering the building that housed the holy shrine, Canto knelt and began to pray. He felt deep stirrings and a powerful sense of serenity. He asked for help with his depression and his drinking problem. He felt remorse for how he had pushed his family away and how he had brought despair to their lives. He asked for forgiveness for being selfish and felt a wave of calmness and tranquility wash over him.

Concha and his family were standing right by his side, all joined in prayer with him. He wept with joy and gratitude.

CHAPTER 9:
At the Crossroads

In mid-March of 1933, Canto's life was about to change. The day had begun with a relapse from Canto, whose restlessness pushed him to go drinking again. He had begun hearing delusional voices again and reverted to talking to himself. He felt desperate to escape his house and decided to go drinking with his so-called friends. Canto never had problems getting these friends to pick him up and take him out to the bars.

They went to their usual haunt, the shabby bar where Canto's former glories as a champion were touted for the sake of calling attention to him and someone buying him a drink for old times' sake. But Canto soon realized that his luster was wearing off: few people bought him drinks. He had been reduced to just being another drunk at the bar. Humiliation was outweighing his fame, and no one seemed interested in him anymore. Canto felt alone in the crowd, with even his drunken buddies abandoning him. The loud, confusing noise frightened him. He tried to be social, tried desperately to make new friends but failed miserably.

The bartender told him that his friends, who had left, would most likely be back for him, so Canto should stick around. The bartender turned to get Canto a beer, returned, and Canto was gone. Where had he gone? Baffled, the bartender went back to his duties.

Canto stumbled along a dark alley just behind the bars in the broken-down part of Pasadena. He was very drunk and tried to find his way by feeling the sides of the buildings. He tripped and fell on the cobblestone alley. Just then, two thugs stepped out of the darkness. They pushed, punched, and kicked Canto, knocking him into a grimy doorway. Canto fought back as best he could and managed to hit one of the assailants, who fell to the ground. Regrouping, the thug and his accomplice rolled Canto and took everything of value he had. The men ran away into the darkness, leaving Canto in the alley, crumpled and bloodied, his clothes torn.

Canto struggled to his feet. He stumbled to the curb and steadied himself by holding onto the light pole. He was uncertain of where he was, but he clearly heard the rumble of a large truck approaching. The noise became closer, louder, and he felt an overwhelming urge to step into its path. What did he have to live for anymore? Gathering his drunken will, he stumbled forward off the curb into the pathway of what Canto imagined must be a behemoth of a truck. *Hopefully this will be the end,* he thought.

The truck swerved but nicked him and knocked him, twisting and spinning, onto the other side of the street. The truck didn't stop, and Canto lay injured by the curb. He tried to rise but lost his balance and fell, striking his head against the rough pavement. Bleeding from the head, nose, and mouth, he was confused and bewildered.

Canto tried to maintain consciousness, but gave up, hoping he'd never awaken again. As he lay alone in the darkness, bloody and in pain, he was inexplicably quiet and calm. Then a gentle hand touched him, the hand of a small child. The boy brushed back Canto's hair where blood had dried. Canto softly rolled over and found himself against the wall of a store front. His large hand grabbed the proffered hand of the child and held on to it. Canto opened his eyes as wide as he could and seemed to see the face of a small boy, leaning cautiously over him. Then his vision blurred again into darkness.

Canto heard the child's voice: "Canto, I am going to take you home."

"Who are you?" asked Canto.

"I'm here to help you," the boy answered.

Canto felt as if he had seen this boy before, maybe in a vision or in his dreams.

Canto reached out for the child's hand and was helped to his feet by the young boy. His steady hand guided Canto, who was walking more steadily now.

Canto said, "I'll never forget how your hand feels in mine."

❧❧

Concha and her family anxiously waited for Canto to return home. They prayed the rosary for his safe return. Canto's brothers had gone searching for him but couldn't find him anywhere. They had gone to the bars he most frequented and were told that Canto had left many hours ago.

Concha, in her nightgown and slippers, walked nervously throughout the house. She was concerned that something terrible had happened to him. He never stayed out this late, and besides, his friends usually dropped him off at the door. They would not have abandoned him on the streets. She wondered if they should call the police and file a missing person report.

She heard a sound at the front door, rushed to it, and opened it quickly to find Canto standing there alone. Concha wondered what had happened to him. Though disheveled, bloody, and clearly injured, he seemed different, seemed peaceful and serene.

Canto turned and pointed down the street. "The young boy brought me home. Do you see him?"

Concha walked out onto their driveway, then to the curbside, and looked to her left and right but saw no one. At this late hour, the street was deserted. Whoever Canto said brought him home was not there. Who could this young boy be?

Canto, surprised that Concha could not find the boy, reiterated that a little boy had brought him safely home.

"He came to my rescue at the corner, when I stepped out in front of a truck. It seemed as though an angel came….," he said with tears in his eyes.

After this awakening event, Canto seemed more content and happy at home. He was more engaged with his daughter Gloria. He sang to her, talked to her, and played games with her. Even at night, when she cried and needed a diaper change, Canto got up with Concha to help her with the baby. The changes came slowly, but they kept coming.

Canto's old self returned. He stopped going out to bars, began to exercise daily, lifting barbells, doing pushups, sit-ups, jumping jacks. He separated himself from his drinking bums. He was compassionate and more pleasant to be with. There was a sense of serenity about him, and he was more loving. He was, after all, not just a husband, but a father as well. He had to rise to the occasion.

Ever since the episode with the mysterious little boy, Canto became more devout. He began each day kneeling by the side of his bed and praying. He did this again each afternoon and evening. He started reciting the rosary regularly, and Concha read verses from the Holy Bible with him. He felt a sense of mission in nurturing his spiritual self.

He began to walk several times a week to nearby Saint Andrews Catholic Church with Concha leading him. He prayed intently and listened carefully to the priest's sermons. After mass, he frequently lit votive candles in the Virgin Mary alcove for his and Concha's family. These were very special, affirming rituals for the young couple. Concha was very proud of him.

After mass, many of Canto's friends and relatives would approach him to shake his hand and tell him how happy they were to see him back at church. His admirers from his boxing days had not forgotten his glory days, and now that he was blind, they seemingly wanted to reassure him that he was still valued. Friends offered to drive him and Concha home, but Canto always declined graciously and reminded them that he enjoyed the time alone that he and his wife had when they strolled home together.

Springtime was in the air, and the beautiful marigolds with their multi-colored flowers bloomed ecstatically in the Robledo yard, which was well maintained by Canto's father, Felipe, a professional gardener. Felipe had several fruit trees—apricots, Santa Rosa plums, navel oranges, and delicious nectarines—that lined the yard, and also had a large vegetable garden bursting with tomatoes, chilies, onions, squash, corn, and mint for tea.

Felipe's resourcefulness and hard work had kept the hunger and strife that many Americans had been feeling throughout the Great Depression at bay. His family always had healthful food to eat, perhaps due in large part to Felipe's closeness for many years to the earth, to crops and harvests, in his life as a migrant field worker. It felt good now to have his own home, his own plot of land, to plant, tend, cut, and harvest. He provided well for his family, and for this new generation—his son Canto, Concha, and their daughter Gloria—now living under his roof, too. Life was good for the extended Robledo family, who never took their good fortunes for granted.

On this beautiful day, Canto sat in a comfortable rocking chair on the front porch. This is where Concha brought him his afternoon coffee and his favorite *pan dulce*, Mexican sweet bread, for him to enjoy. She sat with him and talked about life in general. In the background were the voices and laughter of many children walking home after school from Lincoln Elementary. Canto enjoyed listening to their sounds as they passed his family's home. Soon enough, his little girl would be a schoolgirl, too.

Canto was learning to play the guitar and harmonica. Music was good therapy for him. The Robledo and Jimenez family members and friends would often visit, and he would play these instruments for them. It was something he could give back, could do for them, and it gave him joy to do this.

One afternoon, a young boy among the crowd of schoolchildren walking home from school, approached the porch and walked up to Canto as he played his harmonica. Canto always wore sunglasses, and this intrigued the child. The boy stood for a while, listening, then addressed Canto directly.

"Hello, my name is Johnny, and how are you today?"

Canto extended his hand, and they shook hands silently.

"Why are you always wearing sunglasses?" Johnny asked. "Is something wrong with your eyes?"

Canto explained to the child how he had lost his ability to see. He was able to see before his accident in the boxing ring. The inquisitive little boy wanted to know more.

"Canto, do you think you can show me how to protect myself? I can't stand being bullied anymore."

"So you want to learn how to box, Johnny? Do you really want to learn how to box?"

"Yes."

"Well, boxing is a very tough sport. You have to work really hard to get your body ready to fight. And you have to be positive and believe in yourself. Could you do those things?"

"Yes," said Johnny. He hung on Canto's every word.

"You meet many people in boxing," continued Canto. "Some are very nice to you, and others will be unkind. Boxing was very good to me at one time. But I trusted my manager, and he wasn't nice to me. So there's a lot to learn, Johnny."

Johnny thanked Canto and asked if he could stop by again tomorrow after school. Canto said he could.

For several months, Canto welcomed the boy into his yard and taught him the basics of boxing. This was good therapy for Canto, and he took a liking to Johnny. At times they sat and talked about his boxing career and how he had won the Pacific Coast Bantamweight Championship. Johnny had learned boxing terminology well and understood what Canto recounted in their talks.

Sometimes Johnny appeared at the porch with fruit or candy bars as gifts to Canto. As their friendship grew, Johnny would sometimes go for walks around the neighborhood with Canto, being Canto's eyes, keeping him safe. In father-and-son fashion, Canto asked Johnny how he was doing in school and how he liked being in the sixth grade. They were bonding.

❦❦

While resting in his bedroom one morning, Canto had a sudden inspiration, and that was to clean out the next-door neighbor's neglected, empty lot and build a softball diamond with the help of his brothers and his two best friends. This lot was overgrown with weeds and was large enough to hold a softball diamond. His brothers and friends were all in favor of this new project that Canto wanted to embark on. Canto contacted the lot's owner, told him of the plan, and the owner gave him permission if he was willing to have the lot cleared and repurposed and bear the expense and labor that would be involved.

So that is what occurred. Canto took charge and gave directions to everyone who showed up to transform the plot of land. Canto asked and procured volunteer assistance and donations to make his dream come true. All the neighborhood children helped to clean the lot. Someone else obtained sod for the infield and grass for the outfield. The groundskeeper from the local baseball field loaned them the chalk machine for chalking of the lines. For bases they got rice sacks filled with dirt. Canto got a local sporting goods store to donate softballs, bats, and a few gloves for this project.

After several weekends of dedicated toil, the playing field was finished, and the neighborhood children showed up to play in a pickup game. Soon, neighbors and friends organized their teams with other friends to play against the large Robledo and Jimenez family team. Canto went to the games with his buddies, who would describe in vivid detail to him what was happening on the field. Canto relished the sounds and smells of these outdoor sporting events: the yells and cheers of excited neighborhood players and fans, the smell of leather gloves and softballs, of food prepared by Concha.

In a moment of reflection, Canto realized how far he had come from the long months and years after his accident in the ring, the depression and endless despair. How things change with time, and with family love, with prayer and faith! Canto didn't take anything for granted.

CHAPTER 10:
Canto's Boxing Club and Backyard Gyms

One sunny afternoon, Canto's best friends, Teddy and Kelly, young men in their mid-20's, as Canto was, dropped by to visit him and invited him to go to their beloved tree house, which they'd had since their childhoods.

The friendship among the three young men, forged in their school days, had grown stronger with time. Teddy and Kelly frequently came by to visit Canto and take him out. They drove him around Pasadena, and at times took Canto into downtown Los Angeles to the Main Street Boxing Gym so Canto could reconnect with old friends and boxing trainers there. Canto enjoyed being active again and being with friends, especially Teddy and Kelly. Concha encouraged Canto to go with his friends and relax. The three clambered into what counted as their "man cave" back in those days. Teddy carefully guided Canto up.

In the treehouse, Canto played his harmonica softly for them and told them anecdotes about his childhood, including his terrible, disappointing tragedy in the ring, and how frustrated he felt at times, being unable to see the world. This hangout with his friends was a special place for Canto, where he allowed himself to speak openly. He spoke of his love for Concha, and how she always stood by his side, despite him never being able to regain his sight. His friends listened compassionately, telling him to keep the faith, and never give up.

After climbing down from the treehouse, Kelly and Teddy rough-housed with Canto in the backyard. With his agility, cleverness, and remarkable strength, he could take complete control over the others as long as he had direct physical contact with them. His friends were amazed at his dexterity and body control. They sparred open-handed with Canto. Canto moved up behind Kelly to check on his movements, then put his hands on Kelly's shoulders to check on Kelly's balance.

"No, no," Canto advised him. "You must do it this way with

your hands up, and your chin down. I can feel that you're not balanced."

With grace and precision, Canto demonstrated the correct boxing techniques, and his friends watched in wonder. The next day, they made a suggestion.

"Hey, Canto."

"What?" Canto turned to Kelly.

"Have you ever thought about a boxing gym?" said Kelly. "You could train kids that want to learn how to box. You could teach them self-defense."

"Shut up," said Canto. He pointed to his eyes with his harmonica and added, "Boxing did this to me. I wouldn't think of it!"

"They wouldn't have to become professional fighters," Kelly countered. "If the kids wanted to become professionals, then you could guide them, so they wouldn't get hurt. You've got God-given skills. You could really help them."

Canto pondered this for a moment, then shrugged his shoulders. He lifted the harmonica to his mouth and began to play softly again.

❧❧

Early the next morning, Canto and Concha were having their coffee and *pan dulce* on the backyard patio. Canto told his wife about his friends' suggestion that he build a boxing gym for kids in his back yard. He told Concha he thought it was a bad idea.

"A gym in the yard? It's crazy." He thought further on it for a few minutes. "Well, it would be possible to build a gym in the backyard, but it's still a lousy idea. Any kind of gym would cost quite a bit of money, which we don't have. I'd only be a failure. No way could we do this."

Concha listened quietly and said nothing. She empathized with Canto's fear of failing.

Later that day, Canto relaxed in his bedroom, listening to music on the radio. Concha heard a knock at the front door and opened it to see the schoolboy Johnny, with two of his cousins.

"Is Canto here?" asked Johnny. "Can we please talk to him about some boxing lessons?"

She told them to wait and walked to the bedroom.

"Canto, your little friend Johnny is with his cousins, and they want to see you about some boxing lessons," she said simply.

Canto went to the front door and told the boys to go to the backyard and wait for him. He joined them after a few minutes and waited for what they had to say.

"Hello, Mr. Robledo," one boy said shyly. "Do you think you have some time to train us today? We want to learn how to box."

"How old are you? What's your name?" he asked the child nearest to him.

"My name is Jose, and I'm 13 years old and go to McKinley Junior High School, and I'm in the seventh grade," said the boy. "I want to learn how to box and maybe enter the Golden Gloves Boxing Tournament."

"Golden Gloves?" said Canto, surprised that such a young boy knew of the elite program.

"Yes," said Jose. "I dream of being in the Golden Gloves."

"Well, when can you start training?" asked Canto slowly.

"Today, Mr. Robledo," said Jose. "I've heard all about you from my cousin Johnny. He thinks you're great. I'm ready to go. I have my tennis shoes, a towel, and some gloves."

Impressed and pleased with the praise Johnny had relayed about him, Canto asked the other cousin his name. This third boy, who'd been silent, wondered how Canto, being blind, knew he was standing right there.

"Hello, sir. My name is Manuel, and I just came along with my cousins to watch."

Canto nodded at them. *These cousins have guts*, he thought to himself, *to come ask a stranger for boxing lessons*. He was struck with their confidence in approaching him and their eagerness to learn. Plus, it seemed that Canto had made a positive difference with Johnny. *How could I possibly turn these young boys away?* he asked himself.

"All right," Canto said, surprising himself, for only this morning he had thought such a plan was crazy.

Canto would go on training neighborhood kids and some young adults in his backyard for several months. He attracted over five boxers from the city. Canto was developing the "boxing club," as he referred to it, just by word of mouth. He found great contentment training these aspiring boxers and just helping them learn something new, something of importance to them. At times, young, wild, delinquent boys would come to see what was going on with this "boxing club" and ended up chatting with Canto, who subtly counseled them.

He offered them a way out of trouble. He challenged them to start training, and these troubled young men started listening to him, believing in him.

❧❧

After several months of his informal training club, Canto decided to have a boxing show in the basement of the front house where they were living on Cypress Street to showcase his trainees. He asked his older brothers Manuel, Benny, Julio, Joe, Severino, and Phillip to construct a boxing ring in the basement. They used old rubber hoses for the ropes and attached these around metal poles they cemented into large, empty coffee cans for the perimeter of the ring. Canto asked them to install an old, used canvas for the ring floor, placed over a thick old rug directly on the basement floor for padding. The makeshift ring was not regulation size. His ring was approximately 16 x 16 square feet. Positioned around the ring were 40 wooden chairs for audience seating, donated to Canto especially for this occasion.

The basement was a very confined area. In the corner of the room was a small wash tub with running water. This was used to fill the water bottles for the boxers. In the boxer's corners were wooden stools. One was painted black and the other white for the fighters to sit on between rounds. Severino was chosen to be the timekeeper for the bouts. The kids would box two minutes and rest one minute. The five bouts Canto scheduled lasted three rounds each. When Canto needed more bouts to fill the program, his brothers Severino and Joe would have exhibition bouts to make the card stronger. The referee was Joe Rodriguez, who was a good friend of Canto's. The boxers would dress in one of the two corners of the basement and await their turn.

The boxers used headgear and 16-ounce boxing gloves that were donated by a local sporting goods store. Canto insisted that all his boxers use a rubber mouthpiece, or they weren't allowed to box. He charged spectators three cents each for the show. Concha and her sister Mary made hot dogs and sold them for three cents each and also sold coffee in paper cups for two cents a cup.

Canto's younger sister Alice performed tricks on a big wooden barrel placed in the middle of the ring. She would balance herself while moving the barrel with her feet back and forth inside the ring. This was a big hit in the neighborhood, as was the entire show. Word began to spread around the city about Canto Robledo's boxing shows. Brothers Manuel and Benny stood at the basement door collecting the entrance fees. Julio and Phillip were the security guards.

Almost everyone in the family had something to do with the boxing show. It was smoothly organized, a model of ingenuity and resourcefulness. When the family reflected upon those early days of their "boxing club," they realized it had been an impressive example of the entrepreneurial spirit of their people, immigrants and descendants of immigrants who had come to America with big dreams and a belief in their own hard work ethic, a belief that they could do as they dreamed to realize their goals. Their lives and the lives of their neighbors, friends, and relatives were improved with these opportunities to come together for a boxing show, to share their children's accomplishments, to relax and entertain themselves in a manner of their own making. Their community spirit was strong.

❧❧

On an early Sunday morning, a heavy rainfall pummeled the city. Concha began to experience labor pains at 4:30 A.M. She awakened Canto and told him her water bag had broken, and the pains were severe. Canto called his brother Benny to come right away to take her to the Women's Hospital in Pasadena.

Benny and his wife Mary arrived at the house to find Concha in hard labor and begging to go the hospital immediately. Canto, Benny, Mary, and Concha got into the car and rushed to the hospital, praying to get there safely before the baby was born. Benny ran into the emergency room to get a nurse to take Concha in a wheelchair out of the car. By this time, Concha was crying in fear, in intense pain, sweating, breathing with difficulty, and looking pale. Nurses swooped her out of the car and rushed her into the delivery room with her family fearfully following.

Canto and his family prayed ardently in the waiting room until the doctor appeared with the good news: Canto was now the father of a baby boy, and Concha was resting safely. It had been a difficult delivery, but Concha was brave and strong. The baby was named Raymond Robert (Bobby), and the family celebrated with hugs, smiles, tears of joy and relief, and prayers all around.

❧❧

Three years after the birth of Bobby, Canto was blessed with another child, an angelic girl whom Canto and Concha named Irene. With three children now, Canto's focus on his business and on providing well for his family was sharper than ever. The years flew quickly, with Canto taking on more and more school boys and other youths who came to his house for boxing lessons. He taught them in his backyard and on his back patio. He bound his hands with old socks and used them as a soft pad to catch each child's boxing punches as they threw them into his padded hands in their training. He enjoyed the friendships he was making with the young people and the respect he was earning from them.

He seemed to have found a new purpose in his life. He had accepted the fact that he was totally blind and was seeking ways to make the best of his life by serving others. He was realizing during this time period that he had a unique gift in helping others learn the art and craft of boxing for the purpose of self-defense if nothing else. Many cousins, nephews, friends, and neighbors often stopped by and visited with Canto to see how he and his training of the kids was going.

A New Gym at El Sereno Street

Growth brings new demands. With the success of his gym, Canto needed more room for the steadily increasing number of trainees. It was time for Canto and Concha to move out, to be in their own place. Plus, their three growing children—Gloria, Bobby, and Irene, ages 15, 9, and 6, respectively—needed more adequate living spaces.

In this time period, the 1940's, the cost of an average new house was $4,100. Average wage per year nationally was $1,780. Average house rent was $26.00 per month. Though these seem low by today's standards, these still represented significant financial costs for most families, and Canto's family was no exception. The nation had recently been devastated by the Great Depression, and times were still hard for many people in the post-Depression era.

As before, the boxing gym was placed in the one-car garage of the property. Canto outfitted it as his first gym at his father's house had been, though the boxing ring itself was smaller than before, approximately 15x15 square feet, and there was only one speedball rack, one heavy bag, and a double-end bag. He also had a rub down table and a makeshift shower right outside the gym. All of this equipment was what Canto had had in his prior gym. As before, a concrete slab outside the garage provided extra space for stretching, sparring, and doing other exercises.

There was no lapse in member participation in this new location. Canto's boxers simply followed him to his new place and continued working out with him and learning self-defense. The new gym's reputation once again spread quickly, and students and young adults came in large numbers seeking Canto's expertise. His brothers were still involved in running the gym, and he had other neighborhood men, friends of the family, and others who simply wanted to be around Canto and his boxers and thus volunteered their services. Canto did not find it necessary to hire any help. The gym thrived with this communal business model.

Canto continued to charge an enrollment fee of about fifty cents to a dollar for the use of the gym and access to Canto's guidance. He gave group lessons or individual lessons as needed. Canto's emphasis on access to all and on keeping youths occupied, safe, healthy, and off the streets was still a primary motivator for him.

When a new boy showed up, young and small, Canto always took his hand, wondering if it might be the same hand that had once helped him in a darkened alley. Concha assured Canto that perhaps, in some way, each of the children represented that one child that he would never forget.

While training the boxers, Canto went into the modified ring with his technique of following movements by touch. He put his hands on his boxers' shoulders and felt their body movements. He could detect if they were balanced. He taught them with focused care and attention, emphasizing the skills of self-defense.

Canto had an uncanny ability to easily establish rapport and warmhearted relationships with young people, all the while instilling discipline. His expectations of them included that they must always demonstrate respect toward Canto and have good manners with one another. He accepted no profanity from anyone, or any inappropriate behaviors. He insisted that all his trainees work hard in school, be obedient toward their teachers and other adults, and be respectful at home. Canto clearly believed that discipline should suffuse all the realms of these children's lives.

The couple's children became more involved in the family business than ever, their obligations and interest growing as they grew. Bobby, Canto's only son at this time, competed in the Golden Gloves Tournament, Lightweight Division, and did very well. Canto had begun putting his boxers on the public stage, giving them visibility and greater motivation for their training. He trained Bobby personally, as he did all his boxers. Canto entered about two to four boxers in the prestigious annual Golden Gloves events.

At this gym, Canto attracted 10-15 boxers ranging in age from about 8 years old to adult men 25-30 years old. Because the gym was physically small, and these gym members attended almost daily, this was considered a good-sized clientele for Canto. His boxers worked out several hours a day. They were a dedicated bunch. He had some among them who turned pro under his tutelage. He had three or four pro boxers at this gym. He trained them hard most of the week and entered them in competitive events.

❧

Increasing Visibility for Canto and His Boxers

The boys and young men who wanted to enter the Golden Gloves Tournament were serious about boxing. Canto told the older boys that they must train six days a week with three miles of running daily for conditioning. He wanted them to train between the hours of 3:00-5:00 P.M. on weekdays (after school) and 10:00 on Saturday mornings. He wouldn't put anybody in the ring who wasn't in peak condition. He wouldn't endanger them by exposing them to a match they weren't physically capable of handling.

Canto gave his boxers everything he could to get them in the best shape possible. He staged regular boxing shows at different venues once or twice per month. These were non-title events meant to give public visibility to his boxers, as well as to create publicity and name recognition for his gym. During this time period, Canto partnered with Morrie Cohan, who owned the Pasadena Arena and was very popular in Pasadena, to produce these public events. Canto and Morrie came up with the idea of having a boxing show once a week with half professional wrestling and half amateur boxing.

Canto got the contract to supply the amateur boxers. He had a roster of boxers he strongly promoted: Billy Evans, an outstanding lightweight; Sonny Gill, an up-and-coming middleweight; and his son, Bobby Robledo, an evolving champion. The problem was that Canto and Morrie needed an announcer who could do both wrestling and boxing.

Canto told Morrie one day: "I have an announcer. His name is Joe Rodriguez." Joe had been selling papers out front of the arena for a year, and he knew the wrestlers pretty well.

Morrie, said, "I've never heard of him."

Canto replied, "Joe has been announcing before packed houses on many Friday nights for me."

Canto and Morrie decided Joe would be the announcer at the Pasadena Arena. That started Joe Rodriguez' successful, 35-year career as a professional ring announcer.

In addition to these regular mixed-sport shows, Canto had several boxers who competed in the Catholic Youth Organization (CYO) boxing tournaments. His boxers did well, and this helped popularize Canto's gym even more. Eventually, Canto diversified to giving private boxing lessons at the gym, and even provided private training for interested girls. Many of these young girls wanted to take lessons for self-protection and physical conditioning.

◈◈

Canto was a phenomenal entrepreneur who enjoyed new business ventures and taking risks. He organized and ran the various tasks for the very successful boxing shows he regularly produced for the community and the media, who eventually caught on about Canto's prominence as a boxing promoter and community advocate. Early on, Canto learned that he could make money promoting dances, so he started promoting many dances all over Pasadena. Canto, Concha, and their helpers also learned how to sell advertising spaces in the dance programs.

Canto and Concha, with volunteers from their gym, would walk all over Pasadena selling ads for each dance program. They worked out a formula, rented a location, set up the entertainment, had tickets printed, and even set up an accounting system. Canto would get all the famous boxers he felt would come, and invite them, such as Art Aragon, Enrique Bolanos, and Billy Evans. Next, he would have the programs printed. Canto always had a cause, such as *"Fight to Battle Juvenile Delinquency."* His productions were thus always win/win endeavors: his family benefited, and his charitable causes did, too.

Concha was steadfastly the eyes and "cheerleader" for her husband. She always urged him to pursue his goals, utilize his immense talents to help others, and continue fulfilling his noble mission in life of giving back to the community he loved so much.

These were fulfilling years for Canto and Concha. They worked in tandem to build his business and reputation, though Concha never relinquished her prime duties as mother and steward of the household. As the old saying goes, she "kept the home fires burning."

Concha also made sure all their financial obligations and paperwork regarding their business were in order and precisely maintained. Canto, for his part, kept honing his skills. Many people, seeing him in motion at boxing events with his boxers, seeing him navigate public spaces, seeing him in conversation with others, couldn't believe this was a blind man. He continued to amaze.

⁂

World War II had spiraled into a truly global conflict. Americans were fighting against the Japanese in the Pacific and joining the allies to face off against the Germans in Europe and North Africa. The attack on Pearl Harbor was a violently pivotal event in modern American history. People didn't feel totally safe again. Fear, even in the United States, where no battles were fought, was widespread. Air raid drills were a common practice for the public and the schools. Thousands of Japanese-Americans were forced to leave their homes and businesses and were moved into detention camps for fear they might try to help the enemy. These were cataclysmic times in America.

Canto and Concha, aware of the tragedy striking nations overseas, took nothing for granted. They lived life peacefully, prayerfully, with attention to the small details of their work and recreation. They spent as much time together as they could, especially during the warm summer months. They often went to the Tujunga Canyon River, played in the stream with their children, and moved rocks around to create a small wading pool for them. Canto enjoyed spending the day with the family here, with simple lunches of Concha's homemade burritos, corn on the cob, and sodas. This was a good balance for Canto in his hectic daily life. On Sundays, his family went to Brookside Park to enjoy the natural surroundings and relax beneath massive oak trees in peace and serenity.

The struggles of the war were far away, as Canto needed to make them be. He fought his own battles here in the homeland every day, sightless but committed to his family and his boxers. The peace and serenity he created in his life with his devoted wife and children helped offset the turmoils he had suffered and the turmoils of the world in that era.

CHAPTER 11:
The Crown City Boxing Stables

Canto continued to train fighters at his El Sereno gym with energy and devotion. Television exposure had greatly influenced many young people to take up the manly sport of boxing. Canto was pleased with the new crop of aspirants. Many of them were eager to fight competitively, but Canto began realizing that the gym was too small to handle this burgeoning interest and involvement. He must find another location where he could capitalize on the momentum and look for his next future champion. For a trainer like Canto, finding the next new champion was always a major element of his work.

He certainly had plenty of candidates for grooming. Canto had been receiving more acclaim in the community for his work with youths, and this led to increasing interest in learning how to be a boxer under the tutelage of the popular Canto "TNT" Robledo. Adults and former boxers were joining the ranks of children who came to the gym.

Canto had become somewhat of a celebrity figure to many local residents. Many schools in the area asked him to help raise funds for their student body clubs. Canto obliged, such as by staging amateur boxing shows in the school's gym and giving the proceeds to the clubs. During his boxing shows in November 1950, for example, Canto would give away turkeys to the winners and losers on the boxing cards.

On some of his boxing shows at the Pasadena Arena, Canto would only charge a new toy for admission. The collected toys would then be given by Canto, or the policemen and firemen who collaborated in charity work with him, to disadvantaged children at the local Optimist Home for Boys and other organizations.

❦❦

Larger Home, Larger Gym

Change continued to come for Canto. After over a decade of running his boxing club, backyard gyms, and boxing lessons, Canto's reputation as a trainer went well beyond the boundaries of Pasadena. His boxing shows were highly successful, with word always spreading quickly throughout the city and surrounding areas. Thus it was natural that the dream would continue to expand.

Canto and Concha had lived on El Sereno Street in northwest Pasadena for about seven years. They had been looking for a bigger home to expand his gym and provide more room for their family. On a dazzling Sunday morning, Canto told Concha that, after church, he wanted to go and visit a property on Manzanita Street that a friend had told him about.

The property at 901 Manzanita was a large property, with a wide, long back yard and an old, wooden single-car garage at the property's edge. The modest house would be a step up for the Robledo family. No longer would they have to rent. Now they could buy their own property, an American dream. It had three bedrooms, a large living room with a nice wood-burning fireplace with a beautiful white brick surround. The house also had two bathrooms, a large kitchen equipped with a gas stove, and a small studio that could be used as a spare bedroom.

The back yard was filled with overgrown grass and weeds, with large rocks and boulders scattered all over. The dilapidated wooden fence on one side of the yard was falling down. The house needed painting and other repairs. The down payment on the house would be $ 1,500 and the cost of the property was $9,000. This was all Canto and Concha could afford on their small budget, but this opportunity to be homeowners was an exciting time for them. This house was to become their permanent home, as fate decreed. The couple lived in it until Canto's final days.

The neighborhood was predominantly African-American. Canto now could draw more African-Americans into his future boxing stables. He also wanted to help curb juvenile delinquency in the Northwest side of Pasadena. He had already established himself with the community as a leader and a trail blazer, with a vision for the youth of Pasadena.

To be able to make the down payment on the home, Canto helped Morrie Cohan set up matches and promote them, which had garnered 15 percent of the concession sales for Canto. This profit-sharing arrangement with Morrie had allowed Canto to save money for the down payment on the Manzanita house. In the years to come, Canto would collaborate with Morrie on many other local events, largely community charity endeavors.

The Manzanita property became the perfect place for Canto's gym, now in its third location. Because this property was larger than their other ones, with a larger lot, the Robledo brothers were able to build a larger concrete slab for their sparring platform and space for the boxers to stretch and do other exercises. The property had a one-car garage like their other homes, but the family tore it down and built a large structure that became the permanent Crown City Boxing Stables. It housed a regulation-size 18x18 square foot boxing ring.

The construction of the Crown City Boxing Stables in 1955 was another cooperative family endeavor. The Robledo brothers began by clearing and cleaning out the single-car garage. Canto asked his brothers to hang three heavy sandbags by the rafters overhead. He also asked all six of his brothers to lay a concrete slab of cement the size of a small patio outside of the garage. This would be where the boxers could do their jump rope exercises, and even on occasions use it as a modified ring without ropes. This could be a place where boxers would spar and shadow box.

Speed ball platforms were built by a local carpenter, Art Romero, who was married to Gloria, Canto's eldest child. Canto was highly pleased with the additions of the speed balls, the hanging pear-shaped balls that boxers hit rapidly to develop their speed and coordination. His gym was slowly but surely being built. The heavy bags were donated by the Main Street Gym in Los Angeles. They were empty when donated and had to be filled with sand and foam. Instead, Canto filled the old bags with furniture stuffing from old couches and pillows. The sand was donated by a local building company at which Canto's brother Benny worked.

Canto's brother Severino managed to bring in a 10-pound medicine ball for the workouts. Boxing equipment was donated by Irv Norm's Sporting Goods Store in Pasadena. The owner, Irv Norm, had become good friends with Canto and admired what he was doing for the youth of Pasadena. Irv had a son who wanted to learn how to box and defend himself. Canto agreed to train him if Irv would donate boxing gloves, bag gloves, and mouthpieces, which is what he did.

Finally, the Crown City Boxing Stables were completed. This was a momentous event not just for the Robledo family, but for the city as well: a new gym built by a former champion, a local hero, the son of Mexican immigrants. It was historic in those senses, and Canto felt very proud of this achievement. His entire family and their neighborhood were pleased with the attainment of Canto's dream, for it was filling an expressed need of local youths as well.

With the gym open on Manzanita Street and operating full time, many police officers would stop by and say hello to Canto and wish him well. In fact, some of the officers had private morning lessons with him. My uncle Severino was living at their house, and he often would make either chili or *chili con carne* for the police officers.

৵৯৵৯

Almost immediately after its completion, a stream of local children and young men began coming to the new gym after school. Canto set up a boxing lesson schedule for the youngsters. He was a tough, no-nonsense person with high standards and no patience with slackers and pretenders. In his gym, he was in control at all times. Participants had to pay dues to work out. Concha wrote their names on a ledger that she kept in the house and how much they paid each month. Each boxer paid in cash.

With youngsters who wanted to learn to box but who had no prior experience, Canto would go into the ring and talk to them. He went through the motions of the fundamentals for them. He instructed them how to block, hit, shift, and feint properly. He also instructed them in proper stance and balance and how to throw a proper jab, keep your guard up, and chin down.

Canto knew it wasn't necessary to have an opponent in front of his trainees when instructing them. His unique technique of following movements by feeling replaced that. When he finished teaching in the ring, he also crouched on the ring apron. He depended on his friends Kelly or Teddy to describe what was happening in the ring. Canto then called out corrections to the young boxers to improve their form. He was in tune with all that transpired in his gym, with his acute, perceptive, and insightful senses. He was seemingly able to "see" with his hands and hear the sounds to help him in his sightless world.

If a boxer did not exert maximum effort, Canto would blame it on what he called *"Yellow Tongus."* He wanted the best from everyone at all times. His fighters did not want to be called *"Yellow Tongus."*

Boxers Joe Rodriguez and Felton Jamerson personally experienced the embarrassment of not meeting Canto's high standards. They were training in the gym one day when Canto suggested they get in the ring and spar. These boxers hadn't had much experience in the ring, but Canto matched them against a tough knockout puncher named Chaco. The boxers were reluctant to fight Chaco, but they were afraid of being called *Yellow Tongus.* Felton went in first and Chaco pummeled him. Then it was Joe's turn. With a combination of rapid punches, Chaco knocked him out within 30 seconds. It was a painful realization for Joe and Felton that they needed to get in better shape fast.

Canto's instructions went beyond physical training. He advised the boys regarding diet, sleeping habits and civility. He was helping to form the whole child, as education experts would say, not just a boxer. Canto was making a difference in his world.

❧❧

Diverse Boxers Canto Trained

When World War II ended, many of the returning soldiers wanted to go back to their boxing involvement. Numerous local soldiers had learned boxing in the military, while others remembered Canto and his gym. Others had heard of his boxing club and had spent some time training with him. Thus, the population in the gym continued to increase with new and returning talents. Canto had three very good and promising amateur boxers in the gym at this time who had served in the military during World War II: Frank Estrada, Joe Guerrola, and Joe Rodriguez.

The city's best-known Zoot Suitors were also Canto's trainees in the gym: Ruben (Tiny) Morales, Joe (Jabbin) Rodriguez, and Frank "The Spider" Estrada. Many boxers who fought for Canto were there to enhance their position in the community. He had the elite *pachucos*, or gang members, fighting for him. Canto was getting these youngsters off the street, which would set a pattern throughout his long career.

One day a man from an affluent family showed up at Canto's gym with his son, asking to see Canto privately. The father told him that his son was extremely shy with other boys his age, declining to join them at games and play. He refused to follow directions of his parents and was always off by himself. The son was terribly lonely, said his father. The man had heard about Canto Robledo through Captain Morgan of the Pasadena Police Department. He wondered if there might be something here to help his son. Canto took the boy aside and talked to him. He put his hand on the young boy's shoulder to get a sense of his feelings. He welcomed him into the gym. The young boy felt this genuine acceptance and decided he wanted to start working out and having Canto train him.

On another occasion, a teenager was not following the gym's rules, and he mocked Canto and hid from him. Canto heard him and detected where the boy was hiding through his sharp senses. Within minutes, Canto found the boy and told him to leave his gym and never return. The next day, the boy sheepishly brought his parents to the gym and apologized to Canto for his rude behavior. He vowed he would never act that way again. He asked Canto for forgiveness and permission to rejoin the Stables. In front of the boy's parents, Canto admonished him: "As long as you behave yourself, you're welcome here at my gym." The boy smiled and they shook hands.

Yet another boxer, Charles (Chuck) Johnson, came to Canto because he had been impressed with Canto's skills in guiding boxers despite his blindness. At one of the local amateur boxing shows in Pasadena, Chuck had noticed Canto standing by himself and he wanted to meet this fascinating man. He had watched Canto earlier in the day walking his fighters to the ring corner and had seen him in action by working the corner during the minute rest. He was amazed at how effortlessly Canto glided up and down the corner steps and into the ring, how adeptly he found his way in the ring. Chuck walked up to Canto and introduced himself to him.

Canto shook his hand and asked: "Chuck, how much do you weigh? Do you want to be a boxer and learn how to train in my gym?"

Chuck guided Canto back to the dressing room and Canto wanted to know more about him. "What school do you go to? Where is your father, and can I meet him?"

Later that afternoon, the two met and discussed the possibility of training Chuck, who asked to be called "Charlie." It was decided that Chuck would start training at the gym after he finished his school work each day.

Charlie came from an affluent family. He enjoyed being with Canto and was fascinated with his abilities to teach boxing. After several years, Charlie became one of Canto's trusted men in the gym and at the boxing matches. He went everywhere with him, often driving Canto in the family car to various events in town and away. Charlie was televised in one of his victorious bouts and made his father very proud.

Young boys lining up to learn from Canto included his own son Bobby. When Bobby was 11 years old, he was already boxing in the Golden Gloves Boxing Tournaments and the various boxing shows around the Southern California area. He had a very good young amateur record and won his first 10 bouts in a row.

As his trainees learned more and more from Canto, his success spread more widely, and Canto found greater fulfillment in his work. As this increased, his joy at home with his wife and children also grew significantly. The only glitch sometimes was that Canto overworked himself. He stayed in the gym 10-12 hours a day. Often Concha would have to yell at him to come in and eat lunch or supper. He was always seeking the next world's champion.

Mentor to Troubled Youths

Canto was often called to the local juvenile hall to counsel troubled young men. A boy from a broken home was arrested for some wrongdoings. The probation officer called Canto to come and speak with the boy. Canto visited the young man in juvenile hall and took custody of him to train at the gym. On another occasion, a teacher from the local McKinley Junior High School came to Canto for advice on the development of a recreation program in his school that involved boxing. Canto gave him the best guidance he could.

Canto's reputation and value to the youths of Pasadena was being increasingly recognized by school and city officials. This was the beginning of a new role for Canto. He was gradually functioning more as a teacher and counselor for the youths, as well as being their athletic trainer in boxing. He allowed nothing to interfere with his state of mind and his focus.

He was able to take in any boy in need because his fees for joining the gym were very low. He knew he would never get rich doing business this way, but he knew it was the right thing to do for the community. Also, he charged nothing to families who could not pay.

Boxing in the gym was an outlet that kept the troubled youth balanced. Being in Canto's Stables blurred any lines of distinction between rivals. Now they were merely competitors in the sport of boxing. If you were a rival from the north end or the south end of Pasadena, it didn't matter as long as you were boxing for Canto. There wasn't any gang affiliation while you were in the gym. Canto did not tolerate rivalries or gang fighting. Everyone was an equal, and Canto kept it that way. Any disagreements between gang members were settled in the boxing ring. That was his solution to any gang problem on the street or in the gym.

He continued to work with the Pasadena Police Department along with Captain Morgan. The Captain continued to bring young juvenile boys to Canto's Crown City Boxing Stables hoping Canto could help set them on the right path. Canto cherished his positive relationship with the police department, which had generously donated boxing equipment to his gym, thanks to Captain Morgan.

Taking His Boxers to Competitions

It had now been 15 years since Canto's boxing tragedy. At age 34, Canto had finally found the will and courage to enter the ring again, this time as a corner man for his fighters. All his boxers had been asking him to help them in the corner, to advise and guide them as they boxed actual opponents, to give them encouragement to keep fighting a match. So, with his mind made up that he was ready to tackle this aspect of being a gym owner and trainer, he decided that he would work the corner for his boxers in the upcoming annual Golden Gloves Tournament.

The tournament was set. The year was 1947, and Canto took three boxers to the Hollywood Legion Stadium to prepare for the fights. When they arrived at the venue, he discovered that all three fighters were overweight. Frank Estrada, Joe Guerrola and Joe Rodriguez were over their weight limit by one pound. So, Canto took them to the YMCA in Hollywood and had them go into the steam room.

After a while Canto had them get dressed and he weighed them, and they now were a pound under, which was good. He took them for their afternoon meal in a little café across the street from the Stadium. On the shelf in front of the boys was a lemon meringue pie, a bright yellow delicacy with a scrumptious-looking white topping. Unbeknownst to Canto, the boys mouthed a message to the waitress that they wanted a piece. She brought it over to them even though they had struggled to make weight. The boxers devoured the pie, and Canto never knew a thing about it.

Joe Rodriguez boxed that night and won. He was scheduled to fight the next night. When the last bell sounded, Lou Costello, the famous comic movie star of the era, impressed by Canto's training, climbed up on the ring apron and publicly announced that he wanted to pay for an eye operation for Canto. Sunny Tufts, another prominent actor attending the boxing event, made the same offer. Canto thanked them but said no. He informed them that the condition was irreversible.

•ઠ•ઠ

Investors in Canto's Business

There was a series of investors, such as George Harding, Sal Golden, and Wayne Jones, who wanted to get involved in the fight game. They were very interested in boxing, and the only way, or the best way, to start out at the top was to go with Canto. It was a trade-off for both sides: Canto had the fighters and the gym, and investors would provide transportation, employment, and money.

Canto sold five percent of his pro boxers' contracts to these investors. Wayne Jones owned the "Seal Rite Flexi Liners Company." This was a very lucrative business, and Mr. Jones also employed many of Canto's boxers at his business. Another business investor was the "Talk of the Town" restaurant owner Bob Jacobs. After the fights, they would all go over to the restaurant and have dinner and drinks to celebrate any victory.

Canto was booking several fighters and making a little income on the side. The boxers liked this, since Canto would be able to get them boxing matches, and they could earn money, too. It was a winning situation for everyone. Canto was controlling all the contracts with the African-American and Mexican-American fighters from Pasadena.

❦❦

Canto Makes History!

In 1949, Canto overcame his doubts and decided to pursue getting his Manager's License from the State of California. He knew the odds were against him, but—if he was going to be managing professional boxers—he had to have it.

He knew that obtaining the license required a written test, an oral test, and a hand-wrapping presentation to the State Chief Inspector. He would have to wrap an amateur boxer's hand, then wrap and tape a professional fighter's hand. Fortunately, for the written part of the exam, the State Chief Inspector read the questions aloud to him, and he was allowed to answer the questions orally. He not only passed the written part of the exam, he then aced the hand- wrapping part of the test. He was 36 years old at this time.

Canto at this moment became the first and only blind manager and trainer to hold a professional and amateur license in the sport of boxing in the State of California. He was proud of this achievement. Now he would be able to work the corner of his professional fighters. This meant more money for his family and his boxing gym. He would also be allowed to travel out of state to attend other professional boxing shows.

It had been 17 years since he was blinded in the ring and now he had found the courage to re-enter the ring with a license and thus more completely re-enter the boxing game.

Photo Album

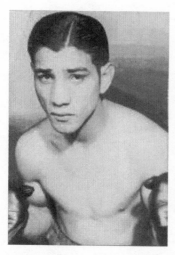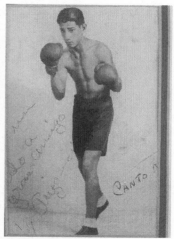

Canto "TNT" Robledo early in his fighting career as a bantamweight boxer, before being blinded in the ring at age 20.

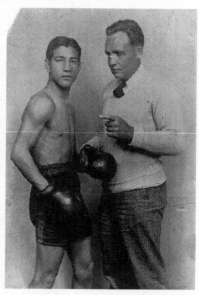

Wedding photo, Canto and
Concha in Pasadena, 1932.

Canto and his manager,
Tom Donahue, circa 1932.

The popular boxing venue, Olympic
Auditorium, Los Angeles, circa 1950.

A favorite boxer at the Olympic.

L-R: Joseph Robledo (author), Canto,
and Danny Valdivia, ring announcer,
1988, at event honoring Canto.

Concha and Canto (seated), in
1988, with Art "Golden Boy"
Aragon, State Lightweight Champ
in 1951.

Photo credits: Top row, left to right—From Rick Farris' Facebook page; from front
cover of program for "Villa Parke Living Wall Canto Robledo Memorial Event," by
Ron Robledo, 2010.
Bottom row, left to right: Josie Robledo; Joseph Robledo.

Canto's Pacific Bantamweight Championship Belt
1932

Photo credit: From Joseph C. Robledo's Facebook page.

CHAPTER 12:
A Historic, Pivotal Year

Canto making history had just begun. The year 1950 was a bonanza for him in that regard. His family and other supporters who'd known intimately the struggles Canto had surmounted to be active and consequential in the boxing world in 1950 as a blind man cheered Canto's willingness and ability to break barriers in 1950 and the impact he was having beyond the sport.

Canto's work with the community youth became larger than itself. His guidance and advocacy of youths, especially the most vulnerable and struggling young men, touched the hearts of power players in the city as well as the hearts of his boxers' parents, relatives, friends, and classmates. Canto's service to youths was most fundamentally a *public* service because it had vital, undeniable impacts on the community holistically.

It was therefore no surprise when formal accolades started coming Canto's way. In 1950, Canto was selected to receive the Orv Mohler Memorial Award. The *Pasadena Star News* wrote at that time: "The Pasadena Sports Ambassadors wanted to recognize Canto for all of his hard work in the community and for one who has done much towards the betterment of sports."

This outstanding memorial award was a big accomplishment in Canto's life. He often told his family that he loved what he was doing to help underprivileged children and kids in general. (See citation for article, "Pot of Gold," in Appendix A at the back of this book.) Receiving formal recognition from important leaders and organizations was basically the proverbial icing on the cake. The real reward, according to Canto, was doing what he did.

Fighting for Racial Equality in Boxing

Racial prejudice and discrimination in 1950 were blatant

in many aspects of American society, since this was well before the advent of civil rights movements in the country. Canto recognized this and chafed at it. He committed to fighting for the rights of boxers to be treated fairly. If he felt his boxers were being overlooked or marginalized, he would confront matchmakers and promoters. He was not subservient to any of them.

His leadership skills were manifesting themselves with the Managers and Coaches Association of Southern California. As an emerging leader in the boxing association, Canto was speaking at the meetings with more tenacity and vigor and fighting for the rights of all the boxers. He wasn't afraid to speak what was on his mind. Many coaches and managers liked this. Thus Canto became one of the major leaders in the Southern California Boxing Managers and Coaches Association, which met at the old Main Street Gym.

In 1949-1950 the organization discovered that the Hollywood Legion Stadium had obtained television rights to professional boxing fights there and had received a lot of money for this. Baron Von Stumme was a matchmaker at the Stadium and would not allow the boxers or their managers in the matches to participate in profits generated. This incensed the boxing managers, and they went on strike, refusing to book any of their fighters at the Stadium. They stuck together in deciding not to fight at the Hollywood Legion.

While sticking together, these managers lost a lot. Now they were only fighting at the Olympic, Ocean Park, San Diego, Palm Springs, or other out-of-town venues. Canto was at the forefront of that strike at great personal sacrifices, because he desperately needed that money. Canto had all the Black and Mexican fighters from Pasadena in his Stables. Canto and his fighters had a chance to make big money, but Canto told the Baron, "Until you give us our fair share from the profits from television, we won't fight for you."

The Baron eluded this strike by going out of town, seeking new fighters for his matches at the Hollywood Legion. He would showcase them, publicize them, and made them feel that he would enhance their careers. Many times, his new recruits fought at the Hollywood Legion Stadium, but without receiving any share of the profits from the televising of their events. These fighters were known as outlaws. There were a lot of gamblers, actors, mobsters in Hollywood, a lot of money. It was a place where money was spent both at the stadium and in the neighborhood businesses as the spenders wished.

Baron Von Stumme, throughout 1950, had been criticized for his job performance at the Hollywood Legion Stadium due to declining attendance at his shows. Von Stumme's supporters blamed television for the decrease in attendees, but Von Stumme's critics cited the poor matches that Baron was putting on. In April 1950, Von Stumme went before the Hollywood Legion Stadium Board of Directors seeking support in the form of a vote of confidence. It was rumored the vote was close at 5-4 in favor of Von Stumme. However, in May, Von Stumme appeared before the Boxing Managers Association at the Main Street Gym in Los Angeles, hoping to receive a vote of confidence from New York and Chicago managers. The Association voted 25-5 against Von Stumme, with four neutral, handing him a resounding vote of "No Confidence." Von Stumme resigned his post at the Hollywood Legion Stadium that month.

Canto and his fellow boycotters counted this as a victory for equal rights in profit-sharing.

ॐॐ

The Press and Other Publicity

Canto was not an unknown element in the world of journalism. On the contrary, he had been featured in news articles and newspaper interviews since his days as an up-and-coming boxer in the late 1920's. Up through 1950, there had been at least 10 articles and interviews in reputable publications about his accomplishments as a boxer. In the periods when he established his Pasadena gyms, he had again garnered the interest of local media regarding his charity work and community renown. (See Appendix A at the end of this book for a sampling of articles and interviews about Canto.)

But now, as professionals, Canto and his boxers were on a larger stage and under a bigger spotlight. Canto was a historic licensed manager and trainer dealing with nationally or internationally famous boxers. So now his fighters were being televised, and the public could see the amazing blind man talking to his boxer in the corner during the rest period of a match. More reporters thus sought interviews with him, wanting to learn how he was capable of training ranked fighters despite being blind. Pasadena *Star-News* reporters were dropping by his gym to visit Canto and see him at work. So were journalists from the *Los Angeles Herald Examiner*, the *Pasadena Independent*, and others.

At this stage of Canto's career, journalists inquired about his past, about how, with incredible grit and determination, he had fought all the top boxers in his weight class leading up to his disastrous injury, and about his present work with youths and top fighters. Starting in 1950, there were at least 13 articles through the end of the 1950's written in prestigious publications about Canto, and the media's attention continued steadily until his last days.

•ᡦ•ᡦ

Canto's Stable of Boxers

He had over 20 top amateur boxers and five professional fighters at this time. There was a series of fighters who came to Canto in mid-career, or at the end of their career. Some were boxers simply disenchanted with the boxing game who were willing to give boxing another chance and chose to go with Canto.

Billy Evans, one of Canto's top three boxers, had been upsetting the local favorites. Billy had made the main event circuit and was a classy young fighter with all the natural abilities to go a long way in the boxing game. Canto managed Evans and seemed to be moving him in the right direction. He had Evans fighting the main event at the Pasadena Arena. Billy Evans, up to this point, had a professional record of 24 wins, 25 losses, and 18 draws. He was a crowd-pleaser and was willing to fight all comers. Most of his draws were considered a win, since he was the underdog and usually fought in the opponent's home town. He had a stiff and powerful left jab, followed by three-punch combinations. He stayed in shape and was working out all the time. Even after his fights, he was back in the gym loosening up, trying to stay in shape. He hardly ever got injured. He received no cuts over the eyes, which is a good sign. He was well-liked by the other fighters in the stables. Oftentimes he would stay after his workouts to help the newcomers.

Bobby Brewer (Mr. Beau Jangles) fell into the mid-career category. One sunny August day, Bobby Brewer walked into the Crown City Boxing Stables with a pint of whiskey. Nobody knew a thing about him. It was obvious he had been drinking, but he was not drunk. He looked at Lew Newman, who was boxing in the ring, then walked over to young Charlie Johnson.

"How do I get in that ring to box with that guy?" Brewer asked, glancing at Lew Newman.

"Just ask Canto," replied Charlie.

Bobby Brewer looked over at Canto, who gave his approval. So, in his street clothes, Brewer put a pair of gloves on. It quickly became apparent that he was a good fighter. He boxed circles around Lew Newman. Newman had over 160 amateur fights under his belt at this time. Brewer declined to give any information about his past outside of the fact that he was from Washington, D.C. He turned pro because he liked Canto, and boxing was just a stopping point in his life's journey. So Canto and Bobby mutually agreed on the name "Beau Jangles" Brewer, because Bobby had such great footwork. Canto scheduled a fight between Frank Munche and Beau Jangles Brewer.

Frank Munche was a boxer from the east, fighting out of the YMCA with a good reputation and record. He was demolishing his opponents left and right. Canto had the unknown. Promoters and managers thought that Munche would crush Canto's boxer. Bobby Beau Jangles Brewer broke Munche's jaw and ended Munche's career at this fight held in Bakersfield. Despite this, Brewer lost the fight, but he continued to fight for Canto.

Bobby Brewer started going out with Billy Evans' sister. One night, the couple were in the car on a hilly, deserted road in Eagle Rock, CA. Something happened with the car. Bobby turned the wheel from a big rock, the car started moving forward, and he jumped out of the car to try and stop it, but the car rolled over his body. Dying in the hospital, he told Canto and Charlie: "Don't tell anyone what happened."

"He was a tough son of a gun," Canto later said. "He wouldn't let anybody contact his family, and nobody to this day knew his family.

He was buried in Altadena. That was it. He came in, out of nowhere, and nobody knew any more about him."

After a pause, Canto said: "He had a spectacular career. That guy had a beautiful build. Boy, could he hit! He had 15 pro fights for me and fought for about two to three years."

Bobby "Beau Jangles" Brewer had a professional boxing record of 16 wins, 8 by knockout, 23 losses, and 4 draws."

Two other top boxers in Canto's stables were Sonny Gill and Canto's own son, whom he had trained, Bobby Robledo.

❦❦

Canto's Embrace of the African-American Community

Canto had several African-American fighters and was respected in the Black community. He was well-known. He had much success training African-American boxers.

Canto enjoyed the music scene in Central Los Angeles and Pasadena and enjoyed going to the jazz clubs. One of his favorites was the Club Onyx, located at 109 South Fair Oaks in Pasadena. The club belonged to The Hotel Carter. Percy C. Carter owned the property, the only hotel in Pasadena owned and managed by African-Americans. The Club Onyx was a natural hideaway where Canto could go and avoid attention. The club was a clean, pleasant, and a cool place to hang out. The walls were decorated with murals by Pasadena artist Kingsley Dawson Brock. Brock was a graduate of the city's famed Stickney Art School and was later known for his famous portrait of Martin Luther King Jr.

The club had a pool table, and Percy Carter had a son named Butch Carter. Butch controlled the pool table in Club Onyx. He knew Canto very well and enjoyed going to the boxing shows that Canto was promoting at the Pasadena Arena. Canto regularly invited Butch to the fights with complimentary tickets.

In those days, the Club Onyx got all the top African-American jazz musicians passing through Pasadena to perform at the club. Some top entertainers were Bobo Jackson, "Big Jay" McNeely, sensational Blues artist "Big Pete" Peterson, trumpeter Clora Bryant, legendary disc jockey Hunter Hancock, the great jazz innovator Charlie Parker, Wynonee Harris, Sarah Vaughn, Count Basie, and Sammy Davis Jr.

Canto had a fighter who used to shine shoes near the rear of the club. His name was Sonny Gill. His father worked at the club. Sonny often would sleep on the pool table. Canto convinced Sonny to start training at his gym. Canto had a benevolent heart and wanted to help him stay out of trouble. Canto understood that some of his fighters had a difficult home environment. Many of these fighters were promising, talented boxers, and Sonny would become one of Canto's best.

Canto nurtured warm relationships with all people he dealt with, regardless of color, origins, socioeconomic status, or any other characteristics that these unenlightened days of racial bias often harbored. Canto valued all people, children or adults, young or old, for his joy in life arose from valuing and helping others. This was apparent with Canto at work or at play.

᭠᭠᭠

Birth of Author, Joseph Robledo

One August night at Brookside Park, one of Pasadena's largest and most popular parks, located south of the iconic Rose Bowl, Canto was managing a fast-pitch underhand softball game at the park's softball diamond. The family went a couple of times a week to see the games. Concha and her daughter Irene were walking to the game. On their way, they passed some swings, and Irene wanted to swing for 10 minutes. At that time, Concha was nine months pregnant with her fourth child. Irene started swinging, with her mother standing next to the swings watching her go higher and higher. Soon, Irene noticed her mother on the ground. The child jumped off the swings and knelt at her mother's side, alarmed and shouting, "Mama, Mama, what's wrong?"

Concha, moaning and groaning in pain, told Irene to go get Canto. Irene saw blood on the ground. She ran to the softball field and told her father that something was terribly wrong with Mama. The entire team stopped playing, and they all ran over to see what had happened. Some of the ball players picked Concha up from the ground, put her in a car, and took her and Canto to Saint Luke's Hospital across town. Upon arriving at the emergency room, the doctors examined her and rushed her into surgery for a Caesarean operation. A large number of family and friends showed up at the hospital and filled the entire bottom floor waiting room. People streamed in with their Bibles and rosaries in hand. Word of Concha's emergency had spread rapidly across the community.

Canto was deeply moved when he heard, upstairs near his wife's side, about this outpouring of community love and support for his family. One hour later, the doctors came out and told Canto that his wife was in critical condition due to a tremendous loss of blood. The doctor said that there was a chance that both she and the baby might die. He emphasized that they were doing their best to save them both. Upon hearing this, Canto said emotionally, that if the doctor could only save one life, for him to save Concha.

Interminable hours later, two tired doctors came to Canto and told him the good news: mother and baby had survived. There was an outpouring of relief and gratitude, and many tears, on the part of the gathered people, who celebrated that their prayers had been answered.

I, Joseph Canto Robledo, the youngest child of Canto and Concha Robledo, was born in August 1950.

Advisor to Other Managers

Oftentimes, at the various gyms, the trainers and managers would turn to Canto and ask for advice on an upcoming fight. Here was a typical conversation:

"Look, Canto, I got a chance to put my kid in with a fighter out of Pittsburgh."

"The kid is a contender," Canto would say.

The manager said, "Yeah, and if my boy gets past him…."

"Your boy won't get past him, not yet," Canto retorted.

"What do you know about this young fighter? You've never seen him," came the manager's defensive reply.

"Don't rush your boy," Canto advised. "He could get hurt. Look at me!" said Canto, taking the man by the shoulders and facing him with his blind eyes, forcing a direct confrontation.

During 1950, as Canto's reputation as a managerial leader grew, along with his success as a pro manager, other managers and coaches frequently sought out Canto to seek his advice for their boxers. Canto was straightforward with advice. If he thought a manager's fighter was over-matched, he would tell him frankly. If he thought the match was good, Canto would urge the manager to take the fight. His advice was much appreciated by his peers.

❦❦

Concha's Unflagging Support of Canto

Canto and Concha were a solid, dynamic team. She had been through his rise to the top of the boxing world and his rapid descent into his depression and darkness after losing his vision. He had even, in the depths of his depression, urged her to leave him and create a life free of him elsewhere. But she always remained steadfast alongside Canto. He knew that without her, he wouldn't have been so successful, not only in the boxing game, but in life.

Canto often asked Concha to cook meals for his boxers, especially before a main event fight. He wanted them to be strong and healthy for the fight. Concha did not complain. She cooked healthy, substantial meals that the boxers loved and ate heartily. She had a reputation among Canto's fighters as a great cook who cared about them as if they were all family.

She supported Canto throughout their lifetime together. She became Canto's eyes for the next 50 years. She enjoyed going to the arena to watch the boxing matches and take notes on the fighters. Concha would buy a boxing program and would take copious notes on each bout. The next morning after the boxing show, while having coffee and breakfast, Canto and Concha discussed Concha's notes and the previous night's boxing show. Canto used this ringside information to help him book fights for his boys.

Concha admired his special gift for training boxers. In fact, she believed that Canto was the greatest boxing teacher who ever lived. He had an insight in how to train each young, old, male, or female boxer who came to his gym. He had a positive way with people. She wanted to be right by his side to guide, guard, and help him with the fighters. Canto understood this success would have never happened without her in his life. He loved her dearly.

◆◆

Ending the Year with a Bang: The Tijuana Fight
Boxing Show, Tijuana, Mexico
December, 1950, Plaza De Toros

At the end of the year, Canto had the opportunity to take fighters to Tijuana to fight at the Plaza De Toros Bull Ring. Canto knew well all the promoters and matchmakers from Mexico and San Diego. He had a stable of amateur and professional fighters who were willing to make a few extra bucks on the side. On one occasion, he was contacted by the promoter out of San Diego by the name of Travis Hatfield, who desperately needed Canto's help to book more fights in Mexico. Canto promised him he would take three fighters for a boxing show in December, not to worry. Canto would receive a substantial bonus for this.

Charlie Johnson, one of Canto's fighters for over a year now, his confidante, and trusted assistant, served as driver for Canto, as he often did in Pasadena, though he was only 15 years old. Their relationship was akin to a father-son one, and Canto felt very comfortable having Charlie, who was a bright, precocious young man, at his side. Charlie— a blonde, blue-eyed, clever boy—was mature beyond his years, and he had won Canto's trust early on.

At this time, Canto had an adult fighter named Benny Cousins, who had a broken left hand but still continued working out in the gym. He needed money and knew that if he stayed in shape, Canto might use him. Also available for this event on such short notice were Felton Jamison, another of his adult boxers, and Charlie, who had braces on his teeth at that time. Canto explained the situation to these three fighters, and they insisted he book them for the event. It would be a good payday for the fighters as well as a little vacation in Tijuana.

Benny Cousins, with his broken hand, was to fight Baby Gutierrez. Felton Jamison was to fight Al Huerta, and Charlie was matched against Kilo Martinez. Charlie told his parents, who knew all about Canto and the good deeds he did for Pasadena youth, that he would be with the Robledo family to look after Canto. The following day, the boxers and Canto traveled to Tijuana with Concha and her sister Mary in the front seat. On the way down, Charlie decided to cut the cast off Benny's left hand, and rewrap it, as Canto had taught him to do.

After the group crossed the border, the boxing press and commission took Canto to the local radio station, where Canto highly praised his fighters, saying they were top-notch and experienced. A lot of publicity was generated by the promoters to build up the fights. Posters lined the main street. Team Canto arrived at the arena and were ushered to their dressing room.

Charlie fought first, losing on a TKO in the third round though he didn't go down. Felton Jamison head- butted his opponent, a local favorite, in the second round and caused a 3-inch cut above the opponent's eye. Felton lost the fight and was suspended to his dressing room. By this time, the bottles were flying from the audience. Then Benny went in for the main event with his broken hand. Canto wrapped his hand carefully, and Benny put up a terrific fight and appeared to be winning. In the sixth round, he broke his hand again. In noticeable pain, Benny went to his corner and asked Charlie to cut off his glove, which Canto approved. When Charlie pulled off the glove, pandemonium broke out in the audience. Bottles of beer and beer cups filled with urine were angrily flung at Canto's boxers, who ducked and grabbed Canto's hand. Bobbing and weaving, covering their heads, the three fled for their lives as quickly as they could and ran to their dressing room.

Then the officials entered the room. They were very upset and wanted to arrest Canto and his boxers. Benny had put on a phenomenal fight and was one of the cleverest boxers Canto ever had. But the furious crowd was yelling, angry that this fight, too, like the previous ones, had ended prematurely. The Inspector wanted to know from Canto how he could decide to stop the fight without the referee. Benny knew the referee would not stop the fight, perhaps because the referee wanted to see Benny get knocked out.

Just then, the officials summoned the police to arrest Canto for putting up fraudulent fights. Canto told them that Benny had a broken hand, and he was in intense pain. Not wanting the boxer to suffer further pain and damage from the break, Canto had felt obligated to stop the fight. The police said they were going to take the group to their boxing commission doctor and take x-rays of the hand. If there was no evidence of a broken hand, Canto and his boxers would receive no money and would be jailed.

The authorities took Team Canto in an official car to the doctor's office, and the x-rays were taken. Canto and his boxers had to sit and wait until the film was developed. Sure enough, Benny had a break in his hand, as the x-ray clearly showed. Canto's boxers were impressed with how Canto handled the situation calmly and smoothly. He never lost his cool and always controlled the situation.

"You see?" said Canto. "The man's hand was broken, and I just could not let him continue."

End of story. The Americans returned home.

It was sad for the group that Benny Cousins wasn't able to finish his fight, because he was a hell of a fighter, with slick, graceful, yet strong moves. He could have gone places as a boxer. Tragically, Benny Cousins was killed in a car accident a couple of years later.

CHAPTER 13:
All in the Family

It wasn't always easy for Canto's children to grow up in his shadow, with his busy life and high expectations, but the heavy family involvement in his daily activities, of necessity, caught them all up in a boxing-centered life. To navigate his daily tasks, keep his business running, and stay safe while active, Canto had to rely on many family members in the large Robledo extended family: his wife, first of all; his sons Bobby and Joseph; his daughters Gloria and Irene; his brothers and sisters; his parents; and uncles, aunts and cousins. Many of Canto's endeavors became, ultimately, family endeavors.

It was a point of pride for the Robledos that they were related to Canto and that they were watching him make history on several fronts up close and personal. In addition, two of his sons (my older brother Bobby and I) created boxing careers, no matter how brief, of our own, earning recognition for our own talents forged through hard work. Looking back upon how our daily family life was so entwined with our father's work, it was natural and probably inevitable that Canto's boys would follow in his footsteps. Canto, of course, was our mentor and trainer.

Canto's daughter Irene, my older sister, was a standout in track athletics. We also had several cousins who made a name for themselves in the boxing world. Finally, Canto's beloved wife, my mother Concha, was the ultimate supporter, the model of wifely devotion, and a good businesswoman, too.

Canto's Firstborn Son, Bobby

Bobby Robledo, Canto's oldest son, was a rising star in the amateur boxing scene. Bobby was a natural boxer with good movement. He could slip, feint, move his head from side to side and make his opponents miss, plus the fact he had a powerful left hook and a straight and accurate left jab. He could hit an opponent from the outside and finish him off with a right-left combination. He could double up the left hook to the ribs with amazing precision. He was somewhat of a sharpshooter. He had been boxing regularly and was having success on the amateur circuit.

Bobby and Canto had decided to have trainer Sol Golden come into the Crown City Boxing Stables and help train Bobby for his next Catholic Youth Organization (CYO) Tournament. Canto continued to work the corner in his son's bout.

Sol Golden, a successful trainer, was a tall, lean man with a thin moustache. He and Bobby hit it off right from the beginning. Sol had some amateur boxing experience and was able to teach the fundamentals of boxing. He was from Arcadia, California, and worked with the Arcadia Police Department as a youth instructor. Bobby, on another winning streak, was performing at a high level, staying out of trouble, and focusing on his training. He was getting in shape for the Managers and Coaches Association Tournament. He sparred with some of Canto's top boxers, including Billy Evans, Sonny Gill, Ralph Lara, Harold Velasquez, Leo Romero, Henry Zamora, and Joey Guerrola.

Bobby had gone through challenges as he grew into adolescence. Boxing helped keep him focused and on track, but he struggled with staying out of trouble in his earlier teen years, especially regarding defiance of authority. In retrospect, some who knew him believe he found growing up in Canto's shadow a bit daunting. He was seemingly seeking his own identity and made missteps, as any child in that situation would.

In 1951, after several months of dutifully attending to his obligations, Bobby fell into trouble again. This time it involved the family car, which he wanted to drive despite our parents' disapproval. He skipped his boxing lessons and took the car for a joy ride in defiance. He ended up eluding the police after our parents reported the car stolen. They were furious at him. On another occasion, Bobby followed the lead of older boys who were a negative influence and participated in a rock-throwing provocation with another car full of men. The men attacked Bobby and his friends in the street, a fistfight broke out, and Bobby ended up getting stabbed in the chest by one of the men, who fled the scene and was never held to account.

Police arriving on the scene rushed Bobby to Huntington Memorial Hospital, where the doctors performed emergency surgery. A priest was called from Saint Andrews Church to give Bobby his last rites. They expected him to die that night. Bobby recovered from this terrible incident and was taken home after two weeks in the hospital to rest and recover. He stayed away from boxing for over a year-and-a-half.

No arrest was ever made, and no weapon was ever found. My brother was stabbed at close range and was severely injured. No follow-up investigation and no attempted murder charges were ever brought up in court against this older Caucasian man. The case simply disappeared. I understand that my brother and his friends were at fault for throwing rocks at cars, but to be almost fatally stabbed without charges ever brought, or without a thorough investigation, reeked of racial prejudice. This was the way of the law in those days, with inequality of due diligence on victims' behalf depending upon the color of skin. The most important thing, however, was that Bobby recovered and eventually returned to boxing.

His training regimen was back on track: shadow boxing in the gym, walking daily two miles around the Rose Bowl, lifting weights, skipping rope. He was rehabilitating and feeling confident again. Canto wanted to reintroduce Bobby to competition slowly in exhibition shows with matches that would likely result in wins for him, to be followed by a main event. So Bobby's first comeback match at the Olympic Auditorium against Al Wilcher in a scheduled four-round bout was a win for Bobby in a unanimous decision. Bobby was impressive in his win, and the sports writers declared that he had a bright future in the fight game.

Bobby soon won another match by a unanimous decision in four rounds. This was a much tougher fight than expected for Bobby, and he sustained a cut over the left eye that required five stitches. Bobby had recently married, and his wife was pregnant with their first child. He understood that he must continue to fight in order to provide for his new family. Canto used his extensive connections in the boxing world to schedule a sparring bout for Bobby with the leading contender for the featherweight title, Flash Elorde from the Philippines. Bobby was very excited about the opportunity to box a world contender. This was a sparring session that other major league promoters would be watching and taking notes on Bobby.

But even though all was well in the gym, Bobby continued to struggle in the outside world. He stopped training, fell in with negative influencers, and took to drinking and brawling. He seemed unfocused, plagued with inner demons beyond his control. He'd sustained some physical injuries in the ring that began impacting his form and efficiency. So, though he returned to training, his heart wasn't in it. In the past, his skills had been so superb, that minimal workouts could still help him win bouts. Now, older and more experienced, Bobby began to face tougher fighters, which was disheartening to him and was destroying his competitive spirit.

∽❦∽

Joe, Canto's Youngest Child, in the Fight Game

It was my birth month, August 1956, when I won my first championship at age six on points by defeating Rudy Cisneros at the famed Olympic Auditorium in Los Angeles. I had won my previous four bouts and had been feeling very confident. My father was in my corner giving me instructions and motivation to win. When I got home that night, I had a tall glass of milk with some chocolate chip cookies and went to bed. Later I found out that I had been voted the outstanding boxer of the night and had won a beautiful trophy with a golden boxer on top.

In 1957, I was seven years old, a second-grader attending Lincoln Elementary School in Pasadena, California. I was just beginning to read books but was already confident as a boxer. I had five fights to my name, positive self-esteem, and pride in being part of Canto's Crown City Boxing Stables. After consistent training by my father, he entered me that year in the Junior Golden Gloves Tournament. I had trained with the older boys in his gym—Chuck Ayala, Tom Sanchez, Jess Orosco, Billy Evans, Sonny Gill, and my brother Bobby—to help prepare for the event. The Golden Gloves was one of my three bouts. I didn't win, but the experience was valuable to me.

Still, at the age of seven, I met Jerry Quarry (who later became a heavyweight contender against Muhammad Ali for the world title) and Mike Quarry (who later fought for the middleweight championship of the world). They were the sons of Jack Quarry and were about my age when I met them. Jack would always bring the boys with him to the Pasadena shows. He respected my father for all that he was doing with the boxing program in Pasadena. He knew Canto would always get a fight for either Jerry or Mike and, better yet, fights for both the boys on the same show. My father always scheduled at least one of the boys on the card.

After our bouts with one another, Mike and I would go sit at the top of the old wooden bleachers at the Pasadena Arena. We would yell and encourage our favorite fighters that were boxing on the show. Mike and I would watch his talented brother Jerry fight. He was a gutsy, tough fighter who fought with a mission, and that was to win. Jerry always seemed to win his matches, and we were very delighted. We were just kids having fun at the arena.

Mike and I became close boxing buddies outside of the ring. We were about the same weight, height, and age, so we were always a good backup duo for Canto whenever he needed to fill matchup slots. Mike and I fought six or seven times total, mostly in the boxing shows my father regularly promoted at the Pasadena Arena and at the local John Muir High School, which hosted boxing exhibitions for fundraisers. When Mike and I had to box each other, we left our friendship out of the ring and gave our all to the battle at hand. We wanted to please the crowd with a solid performance, so that they would shower the ring with coins. At the end of our bouts, our handlers gathered all the coins tossed onto the ring's apron, or edges, by an appreciative audience and place the coins on a towel. In the dressing room, the handlers would count the coins and split the total 50/50 between Mike and me.

After the bout, we went to the concession stand, where my mother gave us each a hot dog and a cold soda. The popcorn machine always seemed to be popping popcorn for the customers, and we enjoyed that treat as well. It always felt great to have completed a match against Mike Quarry.

◈◈

Although I was still a very young boy, under age eight, I was developing new social horizons by meeting new friends and play buddies in the gym. My father always took me with him to boxing shows in the area. I naturally became attached to other adults in the gym as well. Charlie Johnson was one of these adults who entered my life and was a long-lasting friend for many years thereafter.

As I progressed in the boxing game, my motor skills became sharper, as did my balance and general body coordination. Some in the gym considered these improvements to be more accurate than those of my gym cohorts. I was able to execute complex motor movements, such as three- and four-part punch combinations. After school, I would go home, eat, rest, then go into the gym, which was usually empty at this time. My dad would teach me how to throw the jab properly; how to turn the left hand when striking the opponent; footwork fundamentals; and keeping balanced when boxing. His inside fighting techniques, such as punching with both hands, were powerful. He could neutralize both of a boxer's hands with his one arm and hit you on the inside with his free hand.

My father was protective of all his boxers, particularly those of us who were young children. We always wore protective headgear and rubber mouthpieces. Our 14-ounce gloves provided ample protection to our small hands as well as strengthened our arms with the effort of holding them up and punching with them. At this time, still around seven or eight years old, I weighed about 55-60 pounds.

My workouts with Canto became more detailed, including how to wrap hands with the special tape hand wraps he purchased in Los Angeles. He stood me on a wooden milk bottle crate to reach and hit the speed ball for one minute, as he timed me in his head. He had me punch the heavy bag for six minutes, the equivalent of two rounds. He also taught me how to jump the leather rope properly. My training with him also included shadow boxing, sit-ups, and push-ups. My joyous reward after such hard work was the rubdown he provided afterward, even using heat lamps to relax tired neck muscles.

I recognized early on that my father was a gifted trainer, and many of us in the community benefited from his knowledge and devotion to the sport. My father's success with developing outstanding fighters impressed the Managers and Trainers Boxing Association, to which Canto belonged. In the 1957 Golden Gloves Finals, Canto had two fighters at that level. The Association decided to honor my father at the popular Pomona County Fair for his contributions to the sport of boxing. Past and present boxers and other supporters were present at the Pomona Fair that night to help Canto celebrate his honor. He received a tall, beautiful trophy with a boxer on top and a luxurious walnut base. I was just a small eight-year-old boy attending the fair with my parents for the first time in my life. Watching my father be honored by so many great boxers was a special treat. (See citation for the article, "Top Honors for Canto At Pomona Fair, 1958," in Appendix A at the back of this book.)

⋖⋗⋖⋗

Other Robledo Champions

Canto's younger daughter Irene attended Washington Junior High School in Northwest Pasadena. Most of her cousins attended this school as well, which she was pleased with, because it was like a family affair. She excelled in track and field for the school and lettered all three years. This is where she learned how to throw the 12-pound shot-put. As a school athlete, she often left classes early during her sport season to travel in school buses to compete against other local junior high schools. Being a school athlete was a point of pride for Irene and her family. She loved dressing in her team uniform and meeting new friends from competing schools.

Irene was invited to compete in the All-City Track and Field Championship Meet, which was being held at Washington Junior High. Her events were the 12-pound shot put and the softball throws. She was in top form that day and won two gold medals in the track meet, one in each of her events, an accomplishment that she cherished highly. Irene Robledo was maintaining the family tradition of champions.

On the weekends, Irene stayed involved with our father's boxing gym. She helped Canto by sweeping the gym floor and making sure that all the milk jugs were filled with water for the fighters. She washed and cleaned all three of the big mirrors. When our family upgraded to a bigger gym on Manzanita Street, we now had a shower in the gym. Irene was very glad that she no longer had to bring buckets of water for the fighters to use after their workouts.

Other extended family members of Canto's athletic clan included Lupe Robledo, a cousin of Canto's who lived briefly with Canto and Concha while he trained at Canto's gym and worked on his career. Lupe had been training and working out in Colton, California, but had utmost respect for Canto and wanted his guidance. In fact, Lupe asked Canto permission to use part of his name as his own ring name, calling himself "Baby Canto Robledo." Lupe boxed as an amateur and eventually turned pro, with 10 professional fights to his name. Although he did not win any titles, Lupe was a respected boxer who was considered an asset to the Stables.

Another family boxer was Rudy Robledo, a nephew of Canto's who was also training and working out at the gym with Chuck Ayala and Bobby Robledo. Rudy was in excellent shape and won the Junior Golden Gloves Lightweight Championship at the age of 17 in 1956.

Finally, Canto's first grandson, Art Romero, Jr., the son of Canto's eldest child, Gloria, was another Robledo boxer at the stables. He trained there as a teenager, when he was about 14-16. He and I often sparred with one another. He had a powerful punch, which helped him in his boxing career in the years to come. He joined the US Marine Corps and became a member of their boxing team. He defeated the Hawaii state champion and thus took over the state title, representing the USMC. He was also awarded two Purple Hearts in the Marines. Our family was very proud of him. I was close to all of my sister Gloria's children, but I felt particularly close to Art Jr. It was a huge blow to me, as well as to our entire family, when Art Jr. died from an industrial work accident at the age of 36 in Los Angeles.

❧❧

Precious Family Time

I remember music always being played in the kitchen or the bedroom. When I was a child, my father and mother enjoyed listening to various types of music every day, particularly Spanish songs, rock-n-roll, and instrumentals. My father also loved listening to the big band music, and often he and my mother would dance on the kitchen floor when one of their favorite pieces played on the radio. My parents did not have time to sit and watch television, which perhaps explains why our household never had one. I often went to a neighbor's home who had a TV and watched the "Ed Sullivan Show," a hit program of that era comparable to talent shows of today. The radio was an integral part of our household. My father listened to the local and national news to keep abreast of city and world events. It wasn't until the 1960s that we finally got a TV set for our home.

Since my father was unable to read to me, he and I would sit and listen to the radio stories of that time, such as "Dragnet," "Sergeant Preston and the Yukon," "Hop-Along Cassidy," "Green Hornet," "Gang Busters," and many others. After listening to the stories with my father, he'd ask me questions about the story and often had me retell or summarize the plot to him. It was his way of keeping me on my toes.

This was a valuable learning experience for me, for the radio shows and my father's "testing" me on the details afterward taught me the fundamentals of narratives, or story-telling, which we learned further in school. Canto would ask me detailed questions about the narratives, and I knew I had to pay close attention. This was a special time for bonding with my father and mother, who likewise enjoyed listening to the radio stories at night around the fireplace. This was a regular family ritual, all of us sitting together to listen and enjoy. My mother made snacks for us.

What a special bonding time with my father! I saw another side of his personality. He was a gentle and compassionate soul, always rooting for the underdog. This is when we would talk and share dreams about the past, talk about the present, and dream of the future.

꿎꿎

Work and Prayers

During the 1950s, when all of us children were in school fulltime and therefore gone from the home for most of the day, my mother began working as a housekeeper for other families. She did this domestic work two or three days during the week and on Saturdays. She had been a stay-at-home mother when we four children were younger, but she realized as the years passed that our family income needed a boost. I was about 10-11 years old, and my three other siblings were all teenagers by this time.

As always, other extended family members stepped up to assist in my mother's absence from the house. My father still needed help in dressing, so my mother laid out his clothes the night before her workdays, so Canto's brother Severino could help him dress appropriately for the day's agenda. He also cooked breakfast and lunch for my father. My older siblings would also pitch in to help whenever they came home from school.

One day, my father wanted eggs and pork chops for breakfast, so Severino found the pork chops in the refrigerator and made fried eggs to go with the pork chops. The two men ate all the pork chops that were in the refrigerator. When Concha came home from work, she discovered her planned dinner meal—the pork chops!—was all gone. She was very upset and gave the men a bowl of pinto beans for dinner.

One constant in our family life was the unflagging spirituality and devotion of my father and mother, but my father even more so. After dinner, my father knelt on his side of the bed in his bedroom and recited the entire Holy Rosary of the Catholic faith. He taught me how to recite the rosary one day, and I began to pray with him. I can still recite the rosary today.

Canto had tremendous faith in God. About three times each month, he embarked on a pilgrimage of devotion, walking from Pasadena to Sunland to visit the Shrine of the Blessed Virgin Mary. He prayed throughout his trip, which took about five or six hours to complete, since Sunland is about 20 miles away from Pasadena. He began this spiritual journey at 7:00 a.m. and typically arrived at the Shrine around 12:30. Charlie Johnson and Canto's childhood buddy Teddy accompanied him on this pilgrimage.

Canto for years had a recurring dream about his Guardian Angel in the form of a beautiful young child. It was the same child who had lifted him from the jaws of death, beaten by thugs and hit by a truck, in an alley decades ago. The Angel said to Canto, "Come to the Shrine, and visit the Blessed Virgin Mary. She is waiting for you." Canto had a strong conviction that his pilgrimage would lead to a miracle, and he would get his vision back. This recurring dream inspired Canto to walk to the Holy Shrine.

At the conclusion of each of his visits to the holy shrine, Concha awaited him by their car in the dirt parking lot near the shrine. She always greeted him with a lunch and some lemon-flavored iced tea. Concha always packed enough food for Teddy and Charlie, too, and they were very thankful. They would all return home by car and go to the 5:00 P.M. mass at Saint Andrew's Church.

CHAPTER 14:
Booming with Boxers

Canto seemed to have perpetual energy and enthusiasm because he regularly attended amateur and professional boxing shows in Los Angeles and out of town. He loved listening, coaching, teaching, and calling out directions and instructions to the boxers in the gym. He always seemed to have a smile on his face and to be in a good mood. Canto was—long before the term was created—a "lifelong learner," someone who never felt he knew it all and thus, someone with an open, alert mind.

His alertness manifested itself throughout his work day. He adeptly made up for the senses and abilities he didn't have by finding other means to learn whatever information he needed to successfully meet his goals. For example, while the boxers were sparring in the ring at his gym, he had someone sitting next to him describing the action. Also, Canto sat on the rub down table right in front of the ring, as to be sitting ringside so he could hear all the action. During the rest period of a round, Canto would maneuver his way to the corner by feeling the ropes as his guide.

It was amazing how quickly and deftly he moved around the gym. He guided himself to the heavy bag, double end bag, and speed ball area, where he was able to teach the boxers the proper way to hit the bags. Canto demonstrated how to hit and where to hit with proper technique and accuracy. By placing his hand on a boxer's shoulder and the other hand on the side of the boxer's body, Canto ascertained if the boxer's balance was off. He was able to correct how they shifted their weight behind a punch.

He kept up his own skills and served as a role model to his boxers. Canto loved striking the speed ball, for example. He could hit the ball with such consistent speed and accuracy, observers often thought for a moment that he could see. But without sight, he impressed people around him with what he sensed and knew. He seemed always to know who was in the gym, and he made it a point to acknowledge and talk with everyone who came into his gym.

◈◈

New Boxers in the gym

The Crown City Boxing Stables was booming with new boxers, several of them beginners. Canto trained these rookies early in the afternoon before the older group of fighters arrived. By 5 P.M. the gym was full of young men who were working out, hitting the sandbags and balls, jumping rope, or shadow boxing in front of the mirrors. It seemed as though there was always someone in the ring.

One of the gym standouts at that time was Chuck Ayala, a classy fighter with all the right moves. He could slip and slide from side to side and was very hard to hit. He had a good, stinging jab. Chuck fought at the 118-pound weight limit, which is a bantamweight. He was my good friend and stable mate and a promising featherweight for the near future. Chuck and I usually fought on the same card at the Olympic Auditorium, Hollywood Stadium, or the Pasadena Arena.

Chuck Ayala, winning most of his bouts, was quickly becoming an open division class fighter, and my father promoted Chuck in his amateur shows at the Arena. Chuck's father, Tommy Ayala, helped with his son's training and also assisted in training other boxers in the gym. He often drove my father to the various boxing shows and enjoyed being with Canto.

Two other top boxers that Canto was training at this time were Billy Evans and Sonny Gill, both of whom were fighting at the main event level and starting to make decent money. Canto focused much of his attention on them. Billy Evans was winning most of his bouts, and Sonny Gill, who had returned to training with Canto, wanted Canto to book him a fight. He needed money to pay his bills. Canto knew that Sonny was a fighter past his prime. Nevertheless, Canto took a chance on him once again.

Sonny was sparring with fighters in the gym and going to the Main Street Gym in Los Angeles on Saturdays to get more competitive sparring time. While at the Main Street gym with Sonny one time, Canto was approached by promoter Johnny Flores, who asked Canto if Sonny would take a fight in Auckland, New Zealand, against that country's champ, Tuna Scanlan. Canto discussed the conditions and the purse with Sonny, and they mutually decided to accept the matchup. This would be a 12-round main event for Scanlan's title.

Canto received the contract by mail from New Zealand, along with round trip airfare and money for training expenses. Canto would receive his pay at the end of the night after the match. Sonny would have to fly to New Zealand 10 days before the fight to be acclimated to the weather and the food. He would be met by a local trainer and a cut man to assist in the corner. Sonny would be able to train and stay sharp while in Auckland. His lodging and food compensation was paid for in advance by the promoter of the show.

On June 12, 1961, Sonny Gill, 157 ½ pounds in weight, defeated Tuna Scanlan, 159 pounds, in the title match. Gill was the aggressor throughout the fight and held his opponent at bay with a strong and powerful jab and right crosses. Soon thereafter, promoters contacted Canto and offered him a match for Sonny in England. This would be an excellent payday and opportunity at a title shot in Europe, but, unfortunately the promoters cancelled their deal with Sonny and Canto.

Sonny was a natural boxer with outstanding reflexes. He could slip punches with the best of them, with above-average power in the right cross, a stinging left jab, and a powerful left hook. The best part of his game was his strong defense. Canto had taught him how to work his way into his opponent and bang with both hands while blocking punches. Sonny was able to tie up his rivals and counter- punch with either hand. He had learned quite a bit as sparring partner for Bobo Olson when Olson was tuning up for a fight against Sugar Ray Robinson. Olson would specifically request Sonny as a sparring partner. Sonny Gill retired from boxing in 1965 with an impressive ring record of 27 wins, 2 losses, and 0 draws.

◈◈◈

Canto's Charitable Work:
Benefit Boxing Matches at Schools

In 1954, most junior colleges and universities had boxing teams as part of their physical education curriculum. At times, Citrus College, in Glendora, CA, contacted Canto and asked him for support with their boxing program. Citrus was having an exhibition boxing event and had invited Canto and Crown City Boxing Stables to participate. Canto booked his nephew, Rudy Robledo, and Chuck Ayala to box at the college, with Frank Estrada, a gym assistant trainer, driving them all to the college and helping Canto in the corner with the boxers.

Rudy was a senior at John Muir High School in Pasadena at the time. He had invited his friends from school and thus had a sizable cheering squad in his behalf. As Rudy and his team entered the ring, Rudy noticed right away that the new canvas was very slippery. Canto had also noticed this. Between rounds, Canto instructed Rudy to sit down and take off his shoes. Canto scraped and roughed up the bottoms of Rudy's shoes, using a can opener known as a church key. He scuffed up the soles in under a minute, and this made a difference in Rudy's balance in the fight. Rudy had better traction and greater stability as he threw his punches and moved around. He won his bout, as did Chuck Ayala. This benefit match was not just another example of Canto's kindness in helping schools raise money and visibility. It was another example of how competent and resourceful Canto was as a trainer, tending to small details that others might not master.

After this successful show, Canto began contacting various local high schools about having amateur boxing as a benefit show to raise money. Canto saw this as a financial boon not only for the schools involved, but also for his Crown City Boxing Stables. San Gabriel High School was one school in the region that responded positively. Another was John Muir High School, which wanted to have a father-and-son banquet at their site. The school board approved this extracurricular activity in the campus gym and asked Canto to bring some boxers from his Stables, which, of course, Canto was glad to do.

In June 1955, Canto staged a benefit boxing show at the Pasadena Arena in collaboration with local promoter Morrie Cohan. The State Athletic Commissioner, Lew Winston, aided the project by ensuring legal, proper collection of money for charitable purposes and helping monitor the process, teaching Canto's helper, Charlie Johnson, how to handle this financial duty. All went well, and Morrie donated all the proceeds of the show to Canto, whom he knew was saving money toward making a down payment on the house he wanted to purchase for his family on Manzanita Street. The show was a success, with the talented Billy Evans fighting Wayne Cook in the main event; and Canto's son, Bobby, fighting Jimmy Lassiter in a four-rounder.

In another charity venture, my father and a business partner, Art Martel, staged a benefit boxing show at Canto's Boxing Stables. They called it "Crown City Prep Boxing." My father asked me if I was interested in boxing in this show, and I eagerly said yes. I started conditioning for it, including sparring with Art Jr., my nephew with whom I was living in Glendora. My father brought us two headgears and a set of 16-ounce boxing gloves, and I had a month to get into top shape. My opponent would be Alfred Clifford Marsh, my old neighbor from across the street. Alfred and I were friends outside of the ring, but when we met in the ring, it was all business. I didn't know how much strength I would have, but I gave it my best and so did Alfred. I won a split decision and wondered if being the house favorite had anything to do with it.

The event was a resounding success out of the ring as well, with the hot dogs and sodas selling briskly. My mother had prepared over 100 hot dogs, not knowing how many people would attend. She and her helpers also sold popcorn and candy. The "concession" stand was a stunning success, earning good revenue for the Crown City Boxing Stables. Without my mother's help, my father would not have been able to have such a successful event. As always, they were a dynamic duo with passion and clear goals.

Another memorable collaboration of Canto and Concha was getting local merchants to donate turkeys for a Christmas holiday event. My mother and her team of supporters made a substantial, delicious turkey dinner at our house, then served it to underprivileged children and their families on our home's backyard patio. I remember this day clearly. The morning started early with the smell of turkeys. We were in the kitchen when my mother's sisters came to help. My Aunt Nora Jimenez Gomez, Mary Jimenez Robledo, and Mrs. Edna Pollerana arrived ready to work with their aprons on. They prepared numerous turkeys, stuffing, mashed potatoes, gravy, dinner rolls, and pumpkin pie.

My mother organized the team, assigning each woman her tasks and monitoring the group's progress till the end. Next, all the toys had to be wrapped and organized by age level. The tables had to be set up along with all the paper goods. I helped as much as I could. It was a fun, exciting day with all the crowd socializing, enjoying a turkey dinner, and with the overjoyed kids playing with their new toys.

Monthly Boxing Shows

Canto realized that he had to find another venue to hold his monthly boxing shows. He came up with the idea of having a show again at his stables on Manzanita Street. This time the show would be a benefit for the newsboys. "The Newsboys" was a benefit show that had started in 1936 to help local newspaper boys supplement their income. The boys would use the benefit money to purchase shoes, clothing, coats, and bikes. The donations also helped with dental and vision services for children, along with finding shelter and support for them as needed.

My father had remembered the newsboys from his days as a fighter. He would often buy his newspaper from these boys selling the papers on the street. Many of them were poor and some were homeless. He remembered his brothers having to sell newspapers to make money. My father had a big heart when it came to the underdog, and this was another opportunity for him to give back to the community and the newsboys.

Sometimes my father scheduled me for monthly boxing matches, such as on February 1959, when, at the age of nine, I fought Mike Quarry in one of eight bouts scheduled for the show. I had been the 1956 Junior Golden Gloves Champion in my weight division. Two featherweights, Chuck Ayala and Lou Perez, also boxed that night, followed by welterweights Norman Collins and Jess Romero. Attendees were treated to a virtual smorgasbord of boxing talent that night. I was proud to be part of such a stable of talent.

In the next benefit show, I was in shape and ready to serve my father's purposes again in raising money for good causes. I would be boxing in front of my peers at this event at John Muir High School, and my mother would also be present. Having the benefit of sparring partners as part of my training, and the guidance of Canto, I was often in better physical condition than my opponents, despite their talents and energy. That was the case again in this match, and I won my bout by a split decision. The Pasadena Junior Chamber of Commerce, which my father supported, enjoyed these benefit matches greatly and regularly showed up with trophies, which the boxers coveted. Joe Rodriguez, the smooth, popular ring announcer, was a regular fixture of Canto's boxing shows. This boxing show was a big hit for not only the Crown City Boxing Stables, but also a boost for the student body funds. Canto donated his proceeds to Costello Cruz, a very close friend of his, who was catastrophically ill with cancer.

◦§◦§

Sports Writers and Canto

Sports writers often visited the Stables to chat with my father about upcoming fights. He enjoyed being interviewed and giving them insights to boxing. These writers liked Canto very much, not just for his boxing expertise but for his charitable work also. They were well aware of his benefit boxing matches, his donations from proceeds to the various host schools, the holiday dinner for disadvantaged families, and the hard work he put into his gym day by day to motivate the city's youths and help keep at-risk children off the streets. (See citation for full article, "The Sportsman of the Month, January 1956," in Appendix A.)

CHAPTER 15:
The Ringside Bar

My parents decided to lease a bar/nightclub, where they could have benefit dances to raise money for the gym and the underprivileged children of Pasadena. My father had numerous businessmen who wanted to go into a partnership with him on this venture. With all the obligations Canto had in his successful boxing business, one would think that adding another entrepreneurial venture to his life would be overwhelming. But my father was a dynamic, creative businessman, and he felt positive that going this direction was a wise move.

My parents leased a large property in the heart of what is now Old Town Pasadena, on 38 East Colorado Boulevard, between the busy streets Fair Oaks and Raymond. They named their new club The Ringside Bar. The building was large and rectangular, with two stories and plenty of open space in the back, which was perfect because Canto wanted space for a band and a dance floor. The back area had five lounge booths that were quite large and comfortable, and in the front of the bar were 20 bar stools. The club accommodated over 100 people at any time. My father always had two bartenders on duty and served beer as the only alcoholic beverage.

My parents envisioned a place where old timers, ex-boxers, friends, and the very supportive community they loved could come to enjoy an evening out. The Ringside was reportedly the only Latino-owned and operated bar/nightclub in that area of town and probably one of the few in the city during this time period, 1959-1963. Tapping into his vast network of boxers, trainers, managers, event organizers, clients, city officials, family, and fans, Canto and Concha had ambitious plans for the Ringside.

The bar became a vibrant social spot for the community overall as well as for specialized clientele, like boxers. Since bars do the bulk of their business on weekends, my parents created different activities and events they could stage during the week as well to keep patrons coming in. One favorite was film night, when Canto showed old projector-driven 16mm films of famous boxing events featuring iconic boxers such as Jack Dempsey, Joe Louis, and Sugar Ray Robinson. The crowds enjoyed watching these classics.

⋙⋘

Food and Entertainment

My mother Concha was a fabulous cook, in the traditional mold of "from-scratch" cooking and innovation. Bar patrons benefited greatly from this. In her support of Canto's boxers from his Crown City Boxing Stables, she had long since become accustomed to cooking hearty meals at home for her husband and his boxers after their training sessions in the backyard gym, or prior to their departure to scheduled boxing matches. Mother had a reputation among Canto's trainees as being a great cook. She took this skill, this renown, and expanded it for the Ringside Bar.

For events like film night, as well as dances and any other activities involving large numbers of patrons, she skillfully prepared sizable batches of hot dogs, burritos, homemade chili salsa, and guacamole. She made her own chips by hand, from scratch, taking her handmade tortillas, cutting them into triangles, deep frying them, and partnering them with snacks and entire meals of rice, beans, and other family favorites.

Canto handled the entertainment. At the bar, they had a 50/50 raffle and dice game. If a patron lost, he or she was required to put money in the jukebox, and if the bar lost, the bar fed the jukebox. That enabled the bar to always have music. Customers could buy a single song for a quarter or five songs for a dollar. A variety of good music, both happy and sad, was the key to selling beer. Though only beer was sold at the Ringside Bar, I often wondered why I was finding empty whiskey bottles below the booths, especially in the back room. Starting when I was about nine years old, my parents allowed me to sweep the back of the bar and look for coins in the lounge booths. I would usually find three to four dollars in fallen coins. On a good night, I'd collect close to 10 dollars.

The weekends were the big nights for musical entertainment. Canto regularly featured live music, including mariachis, trios, duets (popular forms of Mexican musical performance). He was eclectic, though, also showcasing rock-n-roll bands and more popular Latino performers, such as the Latin Kings. Patrons often heard Top 40 hits being formed in the Ringside. He was always mindful of how diverse our community was, ethnically as well as generationally, and kept the entertainment relevant. Sometimes, he'd stage a dance contest on the bar's dance floor to bring in more business and ratchet up the vibrancy.

All these events were well-attended, largely due to the marketing my parents unleashed. They placed ads in the local newspapers, made flyers they disseminated across Old Town Pasadena, in their neighborhood, to other local businesses, and as widely as they could. Word-of-mouth among the community also helped.

On one memorable occasion, Canto decided to have a boxers' reunion at his bar. My father had actively stayed in contact with his boxing friends and wanted to roll back the time, so the public could have the opportunity to see and visit with some of the boxing legends from the past. Many boxing celebrities and ex-boxing champions attended, signed autographs, and danced the night away. It was a huge success.

෨෨

Childcare and Other Changes

The downside to the thrill of having this bar, which fit in perfectly with my parents' social as well as business life, was the issue of my daily care, including where I attended school. My parents talked to my eldest sister Gloria and her husband Arthur about my moving to Glendora to live with them. They enrolled me in the Charter Oak Unified School District, where I was slated to attend fifth grade at Sunflower Elementary School. To me this didn't seem like a bad idea, since I'd be reunited with my nephews and their extended family—Art Jr., Ruben, Laura, Phyllis, David, and Steven. I stayed with them and visited my parents and the rest of our family in Pasadena on weekends. This arrangement continued for about 15 months.

My father and mother continued their endeavors at the Ringside Bar every weekend and sometimes during the week. Business was brisk but required at least one of my parents to be present for most of the day. Canto and Concha were meticulous about tracking the money and making sure no one was stealing any proceeds from the bar. My father's longtime confidante and boxer, Charlie Johnson, was entrusted to count the money at the end of each day, put it in a brown paper bag, seal it up, and store the money in the safe.

Whereas taking on this extra responsibility of running the Ringside Bar had not been considered daunting in its beginning, as time passed, my parents found themselves more strapped for time and energy. My father's gym career was expanding, which entailed more boxing matches and more traveling. Canto felt fulfilled and wanted to continue to help the young men in his gym. He had over 20 amateurs and two professional fighters. These boxers kept him extremely busy, and he was committed to giving them the full attention and nurturance each needed to succeed.

He used to say, "In this business, you have no time for yourself. You are always going here and there with the boxers to the various boxing venues."

His matches took him to boxing shows all over Los Angeles, Las Vegas, and Phoenix. His absence from the home front, and from the Ringside Bar, almost always also meant my mother's absence from the business. It was a difficult balancing act.

Moving On

Even though I enjoyed living with my sister Gloria's family, I never overcame my sense of loneliness in being away from my mother and father. I was just an elementary school child, and I missed them both. I spoke to them on the phone a couple of times a week. My father was very busy running his Ringside Bar and boxing business. To reach him, I had to call after eight in the evening. A lot of times, Canto was unavailable because he was on the road, or was at boxing shows out of town or out of state. I had always been very close to my parents, especially my father. Living away from them for 15 months and seeing them only on weekends had been hard on me.

It was hard on my mother as well, as I later learned. She had grown weary of spending hours at the Ringside Bar when she wished she could have spent that time being at home with me instead. At this point in time, my family had owned and operated the bar for almost four years. My father agreed it was time to sell the bar. The New Year Eve's dance in 1963 would be the last dance he would promote there.

Canto enjoyed the bar business and how it had helped him connect and reconnect with his friends and other associates in a relaxing, social environment. He also recognized the impact on our Latino community that his ownership and success in that business had. For countless other Mexican families, young and old, Canto's entrepreneurial success showed that hard work and clear goals could offset the hardships and disadvantages that many immigrant families started with in America and that many continued to face.

Also, because Canto felt equal love and admiration for people of all backgrounds and origins, he hoped that his success with the Ringside Bar, as well as with his Crown City Boxing Stables, might inspire others to follow their dreams. Canto excelled at promoting his bar business, but he made the decision that was best for his family.

My parents knew several people who were interested in purchasing the bar, including my Uncle Benny, my dad's older brother. Benny purchased the bar, moved it several blocks eastward to Marengo and Colorado Boulevard, and renamed it "Canto's Corner." The business lasted there for about seven years.

CHAPTER 16:
Growth and Changing Family Dynamics

When I was about 12 years old, I spent a lot of time in the gym. I was fascinated by all the fighters working out. I would sit on the rub down table and watch the sparring going on in the ring. Some fighters were boxers with a slick style while others were more rugged, throwing hard punches at each other. Sometimes their mouths were bloodied, or their noses bled. I wiped the blood off their faces with a towel.

I was an amateur boxer myself, but I was being groomed to be another corner man for my father's Crown City Boxing Stables, though I didn't know it at that time. At the end of the night, when all the fighters were gone, I helped my father by sweeping the ring or putting air in the balls. I even began to wipe and clean the mirrors in the gym. I would also clean the blood on the canvas.

Canto was happy, genuinely content, while he was in the gym, his professional base. That may explain why he stayed there from 10:00 A.M. to 7:00 P.M., six days a week. He always had something to do: sewing up the canvas, sweeping the floor, checking on his equipment, making sure the boxing gloves were in good shape with no rips, and so on. He always counted the number of hand wraps he had on hand because he would sell these wraps to the boxers who needed them. His evening routine was to make sure that the shower water and the furnace were both completely turned off. He would bend down, close to the floor, and sniff and listen for gas escaping from the furnace. He didn't want any fires in his gym.

One of Canto's main priorities was making sure that the seams in the boxing ring's canvas were not tearing or torn. He used an unusual needle shaped like a hook to repair the canvas. Remarkably, he was able to thread his own needle with his nimble, sensitive fingers and his keen sense of touch. He crawled on his hands and knees across the entire face of the canvas, all the while sweating from the top of his head down to his cheeks. He always carried a handkerchief to wipe the sweat from his eyes. Never did he complain. It was his full-time job and career. He tended to these components of his work with meticulous care.

Yet despite this loving maintenance of his equipment and gear, his precision in cleaning and fixing, there came a point when Canto desperately needed newer boxing equipment. The passage of time and repeated cleanings had worn down many of his essential items, but he lacked the money to restock the gym. Every Saturday morning, my father would go into the gym and start sewing up the ring canvas. He couldn't afford a new one, so this was how he kept the canvas in usable condition. The bladders, or the inside lining of the speed ball, had to be replaced constantly. Canto didn't allow any fighter to hit the ball excessively hard, because this might burst the bladder. One of my jobs in the gym was to patch the rubber bladder with bicycle tire repair patches.

It seemed as though my father was always stitching up the old canvas ring. We even tried putting duct tape to help mend the tears, but it was not practical or effective. It was time to replace the old with the new. I had seen a new synthetic material on boxing rings being used at boxing shows. This new material allowed the fighter to keep his footing without slipping, and no more resin was used on the canvas apron. I wanted to buy a new canvas like this right away, but we were short on funds, and it was very expensive. Clearly, we needed to have a boxing show to raise the necessary funds.

⋘⋙

More Fundraising

Canto knew he needed to hold more benefit amateur boxing shows to raise money. He contacted the local Kiwanis Club, the Pasadena Police Department, and the local McKinley Junior High for collaboration in staging some events. Because these groups knew Canto's successful track record of producing such benefit shows, they gladly offered their support. It was 1962 and Canto had been a community benefactor for over two decades. The end result of whatever he produced was always the same: helping local youths and other residents stay in shape and build confidence through the training his gym afforded them. They admired this.

In this time period, the Pasadena Arena, home to boxing events for many years, was undergoing some management changes. Morrie Cohan, its longtime promoter, was struggling to hold on to it. Canto reached out to Morrie, and they both agreed that changing its name would re-energize the venue and draw former clients back to it. Morrie re-named it the Pasadena Sports Arena. Canto wanted to bring amateur boxing to the Arena but needed a good matchmaker, so he reached out to Johnny Flores to help him produce a big hit, then maybe Canto could regularly promote shows at the venue. Canto had a talented group of fighters at this time and felt excited at the prospects.

In 1966, my dad was training a young, bright, and ambitious student from the El Monte area named Allan Angles, and he continued to train him as an adult. Allan became a teacher at Arroyo High School, and Canto donated some boxing equipment to the school. Allan came to our gym three days a week, and he became a good friend of mine. We would often spar with each other three to four rounds. My father told me to never hit him hard.

Allan liked my father very much and often drove him to the various boxing arenas. As a school staff member, he was able to get permission to invite my father into his classroom to give boxing demonstrations and inspirational talks. In 1970, as a high school administrator, Allan invited my father to bring some of his boxers for an exhibition match at his school, including me. Allan and I sparred in front of his students, and they were enthralled. We all had a good time and Allan was a big hit with the student body. A well-deserved win for Allan Angles!

᪥᪥

Trainers Help Canto

The Crown City Boxing Stables were the place to learn the sweet science of boxing. Young aspiring athletes, many of them motivated by making it into the next Golden Gloves Tournament, were avid regulars. The Stables had a positive effect on the paying members and the local underprivileged children for whom Canto's door was always open to welcome them. Canto also had a crop of new, young fighters and some veterans. He had more than 20 amateur boxers and two professionals to train, but now Canto had extra help.

One of the new trainers was Gary Orchard, an engineer from JPL who had read about Canto and his gym in the local newspaper and was inspired to help. He did not come from a boxing background, as was also true of the other training assistants. Gary trained the younger boys in the gym, learning from Canto and the other trainers the basic fundamentals of boxing. Gary learned how to use hand pads, which he held in front of a boxer to teach rhythm, coordination, and hitting a target with the gloves. Gary had a van, which he used to drive Canto and others to boxing shows on weekends. He helped in the gym for almost two years.

Tony Valenzuela was another valuable trainer in the gym. He could hold the hand pads for the heavyweights, which required great strength and balance against the blows of the heavier fighters. Tony had been helping Canto train boxers for about four years. He had brought his three boys—Tony Jr., Victor, and Bobby—to work out at the gym and offered to help Canto any way possible while his boys trained with Canto. Tony was experienced in teaching amateur boxers, and, like Gary, used his own van to transport groups of boys to various boxing shows.

A third assistant was Canto's brother Frankie, who dropped by the gym regularly to visit Canto or to spend the entire day helping. Sometimes Frankie would visit for several days in a row, helping with the hand pads or sitting with Canto to describe to him how the fighters were sparring, so Canto could call out instructions to the fighters. Frankie was an artist, and another gift to his brother was the murals he painted on the gym walls. These murals were large, covering almost the entire expanse of each wall. Frankie enhanced the spirit of the murals by adding photos and posters of great boxers to the walls: Henry Armstrong, Joe Louis, and Jack Dempsey graced the walls under the letters, "Men Who Made Boxing Great."

Canto's business model, since the start of his entrepreneur-ship, had been heavy on collaboration and volunteerism, whether it involved his own family members, as Canto's gym did, or outsiders who were attracted to a communal endeavor. Teaching the children and adults who came to the gym was a labor of love in many ways, and it attracted people like Gary, Tony, and Frankie, all of whom wanted to make a difference in the community.

Maintaining Connections

My father cherished his friends in the boxing world and stayed close to them. Canto knew Henry Armstrong, who was one of the few fighters in history to win a championship in three different weight divisions: featherweight, lightweight, and welterweight. Henry had helped Canto with boxing shows in the past. He now introduced Canto to Paulie Armstead, a California Lightweight Champion, and to famed Primo Carnera, an Italian World Heavyweight Champion. Paulie and Primo both wanted to be involved in Canto's charitable programs for youth, so Canto asked the three men if they would be so kind as to visit the Optimist Home for Boys and make a special guest appearance at one of his upcoming boxing shows there.

All three of them gladly accepted Canto's offer and made a special appearance. The Optimist Home for Boys, a locked facility for children aged 7-16, housed youngsters who were wards of the courts in a city near Pasadena called Eagle Rock. Fight night at the Optimist Home for Boys was exciting for everyone. I was able to help my father in the dressing room by wrapping the boxers' hands and at the ringside corner by getting water ready for each fighter. I also made sure the headgear was properly fitted.

Once each match began, I narrated what was happening to my father. He was able to call out instructions to the boxers as though he could see the fight. He had an uncanny demeanor about him when he was in the corner, as if he felt totally at home. He seemed comfortable and secure, able to sense what was happening in the square circle. During the minute of rest between rounds, he could find his way up the steps into the corner and give specific instructions to the boxer who was sitting on the stool. I was handling the mouthpiece and the water and had to work quickly, without dropping anything.

Canto always showered his boxers with encouraging words during the rest period. In the last round he would have me pour cold water down the inside front of the boxer's trunks. This would make them gasp for air, taking in a deep breath, and this helped energize them at that point. It always worked. This impressive show at the Optimist Home, with the very distinguished guests present, was one of the more memorable shows Canto produced.

One offshoot of Canto's show for the Optimist Home was the connection he forged with the new assistant superintendent, George Kilby. He asked Canto if his boys could be allowed to train at the Crown City Boxing Stables in Pasadena, with supervision by his own staff, who would accompany the boys to the gym. George felt that this would be a healthy outlet for his boys, who had behavioral and emotional problems. Canto readily agreed, and the Optimist boys worked out at his gym for almost two years without paying any fees.

The great American heavyweight champion Archie Moore, one of our most renowned boxers in history, had fought Muhammad Ali and Floyd Patterson in his career. He was another friend of my father's whom my father held in very high regard. Canto kept in touch with Archie, who praised my father's work with local youth and at times offered to referee some of the boxing show bouts for Canto. He also stood ready to help promote Canto's events whenever needed and to make a special appearance.

Decision Time for Me: Boxing Career or Not?

In 1965, when I was 15 years old, I had a conversation with my mother and father about boxing again. I knew that Jerry and Mike Quarry were still competing in the amateur ranks, but they were now in the open division of the Golden Gloves. I had 20 amateur bouts by now and would be placed into the Open Division class, which was for fighters with 10 or more fights.

My parents told me to focus on my education, to make it my priority, and to do well in school. They also encouraged me to stay on the baseball and football teams at Pasadena High School. My parents gave me wisdom and knowledge, and their advice would shape my life. My father still left the gym door open for me to come and work out and stay strong. Sadly, my brother Bobby was missing in action, his boxing career, which had once seemed so promising, now lying in ashes because he had hit severe challenges in his life and was now in and out of different mental hospitals.

At the age of 16, I drove with my father to Tijuana to buy boxing equipment, which was much cheaper there. My father knew most of the vendors and was able to strike a good deal on the equipment. Many of the Mexican merchants loved my dad and welcomed us into the business. My dad bought hand wraps, boxing gloves, body protectors, mouthpieces, head gear, boxing trunks, and boxing shoes. He would then sell the merchandise at his boxing gym. I look back at those memories and now I see what a valuable lesson I was learning. He was showing me the ropes on how to run and manage a boxing business.

After I graduated from college, I sought teaching positions, interviewed for one in northern California, and was hired. My parents were very happy and proud of me when I told them. My father would need to adjust once again to a new trainer in the gym. Things would be different at home without me helping out in the gym. My first teaching experience was a very exciting and interesting year: a second-grade bilingual class with 32 students. I was assigned a full time bilingual instructional aide who helped me tremendously.

When the school year ended, I purchased a round trip ticket from San Jose. I headed back home to be with my parents. I wanted to help in the gym as much as possible. The gym was as busy and crowded as before. During this time, Alex Torres was doing most of the training in the gym. As soon as I arrived in Burbank, I went to stay with my parents, to help wherever I could. My father told me about the numerous boxers in the gym. I started helping in the gym, helping all the youngsters and a few professional fighters. I was home again.

❧❧

Canto's Recognition

Canto was well-respected in the Pasadena community. The city of Pasadena councilmen and board members decided to honor him with a testimonial dinner at the Pasadena Hilton. Jimmy Lennon Sr. was the Master of Ceremonies this night, along with many well-known professional boxers. (See Appendix A for citation of the article, "Gala Testimony Dinner," in the *Pasadena Independent Star News*, September 1973.) The dinner was a great honor for my father, and we all felt humble and thankful for this recognition.

Many sportswriters followed Canto, like fans, and his group of boxers. He had a close friend who was a sportswriter for the *Independent Star News*. His name was Don Pickard, an up-and-coming journalist who was establishing himself as a "beat reporter" for the sports section of the *Independent*. Don wrote an extensive story about my father. (See citation for "Tragedy 'cornered' Robledo, but he came back swinging," September 1964).

On another occasion, a *Ring Magazine* reporter came to visit and chat with Canto about his new and highly rated fighter, Jose Antonio Rosa, who had been featured a few months before as the "Prospect of the Month." Rosa had been on a winning streak, and the *Ring Magazine* wanted to update this rising star. (See citation for "The Ring," October 1974.)

After the Golden Gloves bouts at the Olympic Auditorium, a *Los Angeles Times* sportswriter, John Allan, wanted an exclusive interview with Canto. He was determined to know more about this unique blind trainer. Canto was more than happy to speak with John. The interview was conducted at Canto's gym. The article described Canto's last fight with Hilo Hernandez in Seattle, and how Canto had been unable to see his opponent clearly and punched the referee.

Canto reminisced: "In the fourth round, Hernandez hit me in the right eye. Then things went foggy. I wasn't hurt, and I chased him all over the ring, but I couldn't see him. I knew something was wrong when I hit the referee by mistake." This was said without bitterness.

❧❧

Jose Rosa: Highly Rated Fighter

My father had been contacted by a trainer in Puerto Rico who had heard of him and his Boxing Stables. He told Canto that he was sending a new professional fighter to Pasadena, and he wanted Canto to manage and train him. My father was extremely happy with the news. The trainer told Canto that Jose Antonio Rosa, from San Juan, Puerto Rico, had five professional fights to his name and was undefeated. Jose was an established 10-round main event fighter.

Canto quickly started lining up a job and housing for Jose Rosa. He remembered a friend who rented rooms by the month. He had an apartment available just a short distance from the gym and located in a heavily Spanish-speaking complex. Jose would arrive by the first of the year. Canto wanted to book Jose as quickly as possible at the Los Angeles Olympic Auditorium. This was good news for the Crown City Boxing Stables. Canto also secured a job for Jose Rosa at the local Gorham Fine China Company, where Jose would earn three times the money he was making in Puerto Rico. Jose was humbled and deeply grateful to my father.

My father lost no time in booking Jose Rosa to fight at the Olympic Auditorium in March 1972 against Lorenzo Maldonado in a scheduled six-round bout. Jose defeated his opponent in a split decision. Soon thereafter, offers for matches poured in to Canto. George Parnassus wanted to use Jose Rosa at the fabulous Forum in April in a six-round contest against Hector Rodriguez. Jose won in spectacular fashion with a unanimous decision.

Very soon after this, Canto was approached by a Forum promoter for a match-up with rising star Bobby Chacon in a main event at the Forum. Jose and Canto accepted. Jose felt confident that he could take on and defeat the dangerous, hard-hitting Bobby Chacon. Jose trained very hard for this fight but was stopped in the seventh round by a KO, which caused him to be suspended for 30 days due to the knockout.

Two months later, Canto booked Jose Rosa against a top-rated contender from Los Angeles named Frankie Granados, scheduled for the Olympic Auditorium in a 10-round main event. Frankie was a hometown favorite to whip Jose, and all bets favored Frankie to win by early KO. Jose Rosa upset the local boy in a split decision, which was a huge win for Jose, and his name was now being tossed around for more main event action. The Granados boxing camp demanded a rematch on the grounds that their fighter had been robbed of the decision. Perhaps it was really because too much money had been lost on the fight.

The rematch was set, however, and both Jose Rosa and Granados were bristling for the 10-round main event match, again at the Olympic Auditorium. This time Jose lost in a highly controversial decision. Many fight fans at ringside and in the betting gallery felt that Jose had won the fight by a large lopsided margin.

A tectonic shift was about to take place in the gym. My father had Jose Rosa fighting main events one after the other, and I wondered who would help pick up the slack in the gym. I was sure that now my mother would have to assume the extra duties of running the gym business, and this caused great turmoil in me. I wondered if perhaps I had made the wrong decision in pursuing an academic career instead of having stayed at my parents' side to help with the Stables. This was a period of adjustment, but my parents steadfastly supported my teaching career.

⋖⋗

The Continuing Saga of Jose Rosa

Jose Rosa, coming off three consecutive wins, was in outstanding shape with Canto diligently training him. His upcoming bout at the Olympic Auditorium was a co-main event against top-rated Frankie Duarte of Los Angeles, who had a ring record of 18-2-0. Frankie was the favorite, and won a split decision, racking up a slight edge going into the final round. Jose had finished the fight with a flurry of combinations that had his opponent in trouble, but the bell sounded, and Frankie was given the decision. Many attendees felt it should have been a draw.

Puerto Rican promoters set up a match with Canto for Jose Rosa to return to the island and fight hometown favorite Dario De Jesus, making his pro debut. All expenses, including training and corner man, would be paid by the Puerto Rican promoter. Though Dario had an impressive amateur record, he was no match for the seasoned Jose. Canto was very pleased with the winning streak of his star boxer and Jose's fame was spreading fast.

Canto and other promoters were "raising the bar" on their expectations of Jose Rosa and the matchups they arranged for him. Canto frequently discussed Jose with his old buddies at the Main Street Gym in Los Angeles, such as Howie Steindler, manager of boxing star Little Red Lopez and others. Howie considered Jose Rosa a great catch for Canto. Jose was being considered to fight a very highly ranked boxer, Romeo Anaya, at the Shrine Exposition Hall in Los Angeles, which would give Jose immense exposure. This would be a very high-stakes fight, with Romeo being a top world contender aiming for a shot at the Junior Featherweight Division title. He had a ring record of 39-7-1. Canto felt confident that Jose could beat him, and his prescience was correct: Jose won with a unanimous decision, which was considered a huge upset. Canto and Jose Rosa were now on their way to bigger purses and a bigger limelight. Jose was ranked in the top 10 featherweights of the world. He was being considered for a possible shot at a world championship title against the reigning featherweight champion, Alexis Arguello.

Unfortunately, Jose lost his next bout, which was a co-main event at the Forum with a matchup that included Arguello against another opponent. Jose lost in a controversial split decision against his own opponent, Alberto Davila, but Arguello defeated his opponent by knockout and retained his title. If Jose had won his bout, his chances of earning a bout against Arguello in the near future would have been strengthened. This was a disappointment to Canto and his boxer.

But Canto was moving forward with matchups for his star. He wanted Jose to fight a top featherweight contender from Los Angeles, Lupe Pinto, who was ranked in the top five in the world. Canto recognized that Pinto would be tough, but he felt that, if Jose could upset him, he'd have a shot at fighting Arguello. In a 10-round event at the Sports Arena in Los Angeles, Pinto stopped Rosa in the sixth round. Rosa was outpunched and outclassed in this contest. He put up a decent fight and perhaps, if not for the cut over the left eye, he could have finished the match.

Canto didn't lose hope. He planned to schedule Jose Rosa in June against another rising star from Los Angeles, Oscar Muñiz, who had four KO's to his name, though he had only fought eight matches. The problem was, however, that Jose had not been in the gym for over three months, though he was still going to his job at the china factory. Canto and Charlie Johnson decided to visit Jose at his apartment and coax him to return to training. As it turned out, Jose had in essence checked out of the boxing game.

Canto and Charlie discovered that Jose had a new girlfriend and they were much attached to one another. Jose Rosa and his girlfriend were sitting on a couch watching television when Canto and Charlie knocked on their door. The couple invited Canto and Charlie in to have something to drink, and Canto immediately got to the issue.

"Why haven't you been reporting to the gym?" Canto asked Jose.

Jose was silent, perhaps embarrassed.

"I've got a big match coming up for you," Canto continued. "You have a chance to make a lot of money. Come to the gym tomorrow, and we'll discuss your purse for that fight."

Jose agreed to be at the gym the next day.

Canto had booked Rosa to fight the new contender on the block. Muñiz was a slick boxer who could make anyone look like an amateur, but Canto gave more weight to Jose's experience. At the gym the next day, Jose's training was lackadaisical. He didn't seem as hungry, as motivated, as he'd been not too long ago when he first came to Canto.

On fight night, Jose Rosa looked good for the first three rounds. Then, in the fourth, he was clipped with a solid right cross and an accurate double left hook to the body and head that sent Jose down for the count. He never recovered, and the fight was stopped. This was the end to Jose Rosa's professional boxing career.

CHAPTER 17:
Heavyweights and a Lightweight

Canto moved on from the disappointment with Jose Rosa. Always the innovator, the risk-taker, my father looked for ways to diversify his stable of boxers, to mix the young and seasoned, the small and heavy boxers. He was fully competent with all of them. His gym was virtually exploding with new talent. In 1965, he had over 15 amateur boxers who were beginning to make some noise on the amateur level. His top four—three heavyweights and a new lightweight—had been winning their matches and were gaining popularity in and around the boxing circle. Canto focused much energy and time in giving them the limelight.

❧❧

Canto's trio of heavyweights included Doug Spires, Wayne Kindred, and Henry Culpepper. They were all young boxers, local boys with little experience, but he saw much potential in them and trained them hard. All three played football for local schools. He needed to get these young men some amateur bouts, and victories, before they were ready to turn professional. He was happy with their progress and enjoyed having them around.

Doug Spires was about 20 years old, an Army veteran who had learned boxing while in the military. He was a star football player at the local Muir High School in 1964 and had been the Most Valuable Player in the entire football league. He attended Pasadena City College in 1965 and boxed at Canto's Stables for about a year. He weighed 200 pounds when he first started at the Stables and was the first of the three heavyweights to be entered in the 1965 Golden Gloves Novice bracket. Canto had Doug in good condition, ready to compete. Doug had been sparring with the other heavyweights, Wayne and Henry, and having some battles with them in the ring. He wanted to be the top dog in the gym, but Wayne and Henry were very competitive rivals. They were all good friends outside of the ring, and did their road work together around the Rose Bowl.

Doug Spires won three fights in a row to win the Far West Golden Gloves championship. He went on to win the 1965 Novice Heavyweight Golden Gloves Championship. Canto was very proud of Doug, for his victory was the so-called big feather in Canto's cap. Canto's gym had not had heavyweight contenders for about 10 years. Unfortunately for Canto, however, Doug was not at the Stables for very long. He completed his junior college education soon thereafter and moved out of state.

Canto now had more time to devote to Wayne Kindred and Henry Culpepper. Henry was about 16-17 years old, and Wayne was about 18. Wayne was working and boxing fulltime. He had first come to Canto as an amateur but turned pro under a contract with Canto after compiling 10-15 fights. As he trained them rigorously, with regular sparring against one another and plenty of roadwork in addition to their speed and focus work in the gym, Canto aimed to get them fully ready for the next Golden Gloves Tournament. But Canto needed to expose his boxers to amateur competition beforehand. The Olympic Auditorium staged boxing shows twice a month during this time period, and this venue would be a solid chance for Canto's fighters to gain valuable experience in the public ring.

Canto scheduled these two fighters into the boxing shows. Wayne Kindred knocked out Ageil Greter in the first round in a scheduled three-round match. Henry Culpepper won a unanimous decision over Frank Keers. Both of these victories were big wins for Canto's fighters. Both made it all the way to the championship match. Wayne lost by a decision to Clay Hodges in three rounds.

Henry Culpepper won the championship novice division by defeating John Sanders by knockout in the second round. Culpepper, who weighed about 200 pounds, had played football at Pasadena City College and had taken up boxing at about the same time as his friend Wayne. Culpepper only fought amateur matches and never turned pro. However, he won the Golden Gloves Championship. He moved to New York shortly thereafter, and we never heard from him again.

Canto and Wayne Kindred signed a professional boxing contract in 1966 for the next five years, with my father as manager. Canto and Wayne had a very close relationship. Wayne respected Canto and followed his lead when it came to boxing. Wayne was a top prospect in the heavyweight division, and there were many managers who would have liked to steal Wayne away. They would "buzz" the fighter and try to convince him to go with another trainer, manager, or even a promoter. But my father was vigilant with Wayne and kept him booked for fights, which helped Wayne's reputation and earning power.

In October 1966, Wayne was scheduled to fight L.J. Wheeler, a 260-pound, six-foot-eight tall heavyweight from Seattle, Washington. Wayne stopped Wheeler in the sixth round, earning the ring name "The Giant Killer." This made both Wayne and my father very proud.

Months later, in 1967, Wayne was matched with big boxer Matt Blow, a rising star from the East Coast, for another bout at the Olympic Auditorium. Matt had an outstanding record of 5 wins, 3 by KO, and 1 loss. Wayne was in good shape and was eager to fight this out-of-towner. This would be a 10-round main event, Wayne's big chance to upset the heavy favorite whom everyone expected to knock Wayne out. Stunningly, Wayne Kindred toughed out the entire match and won a unanimous decision over Matt Blow. This was a huge victory for Canto's Stables.

Word about Wayne started circulating in boxing circles. Soon thereafter, in 1967, Canto was contacted by Silver Slipper Sports Management from Las Vegas. They were interested in scheduling a main event bout against a world contender named Zora Folley. He had fought Muhammad Ali and lost, and he was now looking to make a comeback. Canto and Wayne accepted the offer and looked forward to taking on a world contender. It was a tough fight, and Wayne put forth his bravest effort. However, he lost to Folley in a split decision. After the fight, Folley came into the dressing room and said to Wayne: "If you stick to it, you'll be the next heavyweight champion of the world." Canto and Wayne took that as a major compliment.

In July 1968, Wayne was scheduled to fight another contender, the quickly rising heavyweight, Kenny Norton. The Crown City

Boxing Stables management and trainers had been preparing for an opportunity like this for several months. Canto took Wayne on the hand pads and worked on his combinations. He showed him infighting techniques, and taught him how to hold and punch while on the inside. He also taught Wayne the double left hook, one to the body, the other to the head. Canto subjected Wayne to countless hours of sweating in the gym, working out at the heavy bag, the double-end bag, and the speed ball. Wayne spent hours on road work as well, and did thousands of sit-ups and push-ups.

But Canto was concerned about the relatively long absence Wayne had recently had from the boxing ring, due to an ear infection that had kept him away from sparring or competing. Canto was understandably hesitant to take this fight and wanted more time to prepare Wayne, especially against such a top-caliber boxer like Ken Norton. But Wayne felt ready, so both Canto and he decided to proceed and booked the fight.

Wayne lost to Norton in the sixth round. The fight was stopped by the referee. Wayne Kindred fought as a pro for Canto for about five years, then retired from boxing, and devoted himself to a long career as a high school security guard.

৵৵

Canto had another trainer helping with these "big boys," and this freed him up to give more attention to his newest lightweight star, Eric Thomas, to whom Canto gave the colorful ring name, "Baby Cassius." Canto understood that Eric could now round off his professional stables with three heavyweights and a lightweight fighter. Eric was a fast, highly talented young prospect who had attained some amateur boxing experience at the Olympic Auditorium through Canto's bookings and compiled a record of 12 wins and 1 loss.

In 1966, Canto and Eric Thomas had gone to the State Athletic Boxing Commission to sign a professional boxing contract for five years. The fighter would receive 66 2/3 percent and Canto 33 1/3 percent of the fight purse. As a manager, Canto would have to get him a fight within 90 days. He would provide training and paid expenses, which would be repaid after his fights. Then Canto would have to find a suitable opponent for Baby Cassius, who wanted to fight as soon as possible. He was in top shape and could go four rounds.

Accordingly, in March 1967, Canto booked Baby Cassius to fight a tough, up-and-coming Mexican-American prospect by the name of Ruben Navarro, who had a record of 3 wins and 1 draw. Ruben was a local fighter out of East Los Angeles, and a favorite to win over Baby Cassius. The semi wind-up was scheduled for six rounds at the Olympic Auditorium. The weight limit was 135 pounds in the lightweight class. The fight was a tossup; many liked the way Baby Cassius fought with his graceful movements and quick three-part combinations, but Navarro was stronger and more accurate with his punches. He seemed to be a bit more aggressive in the last 30 seconds of the round to win it. Baby Cassius lost in a split decision to Ruben Navarro.

Baby Cassius returned to training hard in the gym, trying to shed a few pounds he had picked up since his last fight. Canto's confidence in Eric was still strong. He believed Eric was a very good fighter and wanted to keep moving him onto the main event stage. But Baby Cassius needed to get in top shape if wanted to fight any of the local contenders. One day, Canto and Baby Cassius had their opportunity to do this.

In 1967, Don Chargin, a local matchmaker/promoter at Olympic Auditorium who knew Canto well, phoned him with an offer of a possible match with one of Jackie McCoy's fighters, Jimmy Robertson. Jimmy had an extensive and impressive ring record with over 30 fights. He was a Caucasian fighter from Santa Ana, and McCoy was his trainer and manager.

"If you take this fight, Baby Cassius will be the underdog in the match," Chargin told Canto. "It'll be a 10-rounder."

This would be at the lightweight division. Chargin really liked Canto and made sure he compensated him well. The fight was scheduled for May at the Grand Olympic Auditorium.

Baby Cassius fought a very good fight and seemed to be winning when he suffered a deep gash over his right eye and was unable to continue. The ring doctor ended the fight in the seventh round, and Baby Cassius lost on points to Jimmy Robertson.

꙰꙰

Navigating the Bureaucracy

I can remember on one occasion at home when my father was on the phone with someone from the Olympic negotiating a fight. I happened to be in the front room when I heard my father's voice get loud. I could see he was very upset. He slammed the phone down and called for me.

"What is it, dad?" I asked, concerned.

"Drive me to Olympic Auditorium," he said briskly. "I gotta go talk to someone."

At the Olympic, we trudged up to the second floor where the offices were located. By this time my dad had settled down and seemed much more relaxed. We walked into Don Chargin's office.

My father said to Don and the other men in the office: "Who was the son of a bitch that called me an asshole over the telephone?"

No one answered. The room fell silent, and Canto waited for an answer, glowering.

Finally, everyone began talking at once and basically tried to exculpate themselves.

"Sorry, Canto. It's a misunderstanding."

"We weren't calling you that," someone said. "We were calling that name to someone else who happened to be in the room at the time."

"Yes, please accept our apologies, Canto," someone else added.

When my father and I left the office that day, we did not leave empty-handed. My father left with a contract for Baby Cassius to fight on the next boxing show. Perhaps the excuses the men made in that office were true; perhaps not. But I learned that standing up for yourself and taking the offensive if needed helps put you in a better negotiating position.

A fascinating and insightful article written by William O' Neil, in *Boxing Illustrated* in 1968 described Canto as a man of many visions, a hard-working man without any regrets in his life. Canto described himself in that article as the luckiest man on earth. This article had been a great opportunity for Canto and his stables to gain national exposure. Canto had worked very hard to keep his contracted boxers, Wayne Kindred and Eric Thomas, in good condition, and always focused on getting the right fights for them. Canto understood that his new contenders were on the brink of stardom. He had to get the right fights and exposure for his fighters. To these ends, he navigated bureaucracy with his whole heart behind it and worked as well as he could with Don Chargin and other fight arena officials, Aileen Eaton and George Parnassus, in lining up the right opponents for his fighters.

According to Don, he always considered Canto an amazing man. He was impressed with how Canto would work the corner of his fighters in the ring, and he always looked forward to having Canto visit him in his office. So whether there were any outbursts or not, whether something was said on the phone or not, Don and Canto worked hand in glove to bring success to their fighters.

"And I'll tell you, Canto was a great guy," Don told me once, long after that office visit. "Not a good guy. He was a *great* guy! I have a picture on my wall of your dad at my home."

He smiled at the recollection.

"I have a great picture of Canto in the corner. Oh boy, he was right into that fight, not talking about what a heck of a fighter he himself was."

CHAPTER 18:
Good News, Bad News

In 1970, Canto received a call from the Jules Stein Eye Institute at UCLA about restoring his eyesight. Medical professionals there had read about him in the newspapers and wanted to help him. This day is indelibly marked in my memory: My father, mother, and I drove to the UCLA campus to have my father's eyes examined to see if his vision could be given back to him. We were very excited but apprehensive, for my parents had already had their hopes raised in the past, only to be dashed when medicine could not perform the miracle my father needed.

My father prayed the rosary on the way to UCLA. My mother and I sat close together and prayed fervently while waiting in the foyer with my father. After one hour, the doctors summoned him into the examination room, and my mother was not allowed to go in with him. He needed her by his side and was very disappointed. My mother and I waited patiently in the outer area, hoping and praying all would go well.

After several hours of having his eyes examined, my father came out with the nurse, and he waited with us. He had a bandage around his head that covered his eyes. After a few minutes, the doctor emerged to give us his full report. First, he told us that Canto's eyes were damaged beyond repair. Next, he said that the optic nerve was damaged in both eyes and a tremendous amount of scar tissue had built up around the back of the eye where the optic nerve is located. Third, he said an operation to try to undo this damage might cause death. They just didn't have enough experience dealing with this type of injury to the eyes, but they told us to not give up hope. They were making strides in repairing optic nerve damage. Hopefully, in 5-10 years, they would be able to help him with an eye transplant.

We left UCLA feeling sad but somewhat hopeful that maybe, just maybe, there would be a miracle one day, and Canto would be able to see the world again. With a heavy heart but with unquestioning faith that all good things come to those who wait, Canto and all of us headed home.

∽⪦⪧

The March of Time

Around 1975, my father began expressing to us that he wasn't feeling well and that he might retire. He was 62 years old and starting to slow down a bit after all these decades in the sport. I think he wanted me to come back home from San Jose and help in the gym full-time.

I told him, "Just be patient, Dad. After this teaching year, I'll come home to help."

Canto's pace as he moved around the gym was not as brisk as it used to be. He tired more easily, and he struggled to do tasks he enjoyed, like sewing the canvas of the ring. He was noticeably slowing down. More often than not, he was content to just stay home, even when there was a big fight in town. He usually preferred just to be with my mother.

Canto and Concha were inseparable. Their devotion to one another was a supreme joy for us, the family, to witness. My mother took very good care of Canto, and not just regarding his physical health. She always made sure, for example, that he was well-dressed from top to bottom: his clothes, his socks, and down to his beloved wing-tip leather shoes. Canto had always been a sharp dresser, since his teen years. He was meticulous about his clothes and insisted on wearing only the best quality. My mother understood his tastes and bought him the best on the market that they could afford. As my father aged, these things didn't change: him wanting to look sharp, and my mother equally wanting him to look classy anywhere in the public sphere—fight arenas, school fundraisers, or leisurely outings with family and friends. My mother understood that pride in his appearance helped Canto's well-being, and she attended to this need with as much conscientiousness as she tended to Canto's daily care.

I never feared that Canto was not in the best of hands. Not just my unwavering mother, but my sisters were omnipresent sources of support for Canto. Gloria, the firstborn, was never far from our dad.

She regularly checked up on him, came by to take him to her home for a visit, and never lost patience with him. My other sister Irene was likewise everpresent. Seeing Canto slowing down in this time period tugged at my heart. I wanted to stay in Pasadena and help him. I felt sad, for I knew he and the gym needed me, yet I also knew that Canto didn't lack for care otherwise and that he had trusty trainers in his gym.

Still, I really didn't want to go back to San Jose, the home of my new career now, but I was obligated to because I had signed a teaching contract for the coming school year. The school, the children, needed me. My mother recognized this fully.

"Teaching school is your career now, my son," she said in her comforting voice. "You belong with the children. You must go forward with your education and teaching."

Her heart was in this counsel. Though she loved Canto and knew that not just he, but she as well, could use extra help with the family business, she still wanted me to forge my own direction and create my own identity: helping others, as they had done and were doing, but helping youths in my own way. I cherished her faith in me.

Fundraisers for Canvas and Kids

Canto was slowing down, but he was nowhere near hanging up his gloves and retiring. For the last four months, he had been in regular contact with Pasadena City College officials regarding his participation in the upcoming Cinco de Mayo celebration, which would include a day of athletics with track and field exhibitions and with boxing matches in their Horrell Football Stadium. School officials wanted Canto to help promote boxing matches and specifically requested Wayne Kindred and Eddie Garner for a three-round heavyweight match. Canto agreed to do this.

I was very involved and helped my dad promote the boxing show. I was scheduled to be boxing on the card. I was in good shape, was sparring every other day, and was ready to fight a three-rounder. My opponent didn't show up, however, so I ended up refereeing the matches. I was disappointed at first, because a lot of my friends were in the audience, and I had wanted to box in front of them. It all worked out well. The pro boxers Jose Rosa and Jan Beijer served as judges for the matches.

My father had contacted the *Independent Star News* to run an ad in the paper regarding the new canvas our gym's ring needed, hoping the public might contribute donations. I knew that getting a new canvas was a high priority for my father. I found out where to buy one, drove with my father to Los Angeles to purchase it, and paid half of its cost as a down payment. Next, we had to raise enough money in the next boxing show to pay off the remaining balance.

We had been granted permission to have a boxing match at the local McKinley Junior High School and had scheduled this as our next event. Canto was very excited about the show. He planned about 12 bouts and a couple of exhibition matches. My mother, my Aunt Nora, and my sisters Irene and Gloria ran the concession area. They had hot dogs, chips, candy, water, sodas, and some purchased, packaged pre-made popcorn. They were able to raise the needed amount to pay the balance on the canvas. The show, overall, was a big success.

In 1978, another local school, Pasadena High School, called upon my father to assist them in raising funds for their Black Student Union, a school club aimed at promoting pride and esteem in its students. Their approved fundraising event was called "The All-Star Boxing Show," a 15-bout extravaganza. Three boxing stars attended the event and signed autographs for an adoring crowd: World Featherweight Champion Danny "Little Red" Lopez, plus the seventh-ranked Flyweight in the world, Alberto "Superfly" Sandoval, and his brother, the Amateur Athletic Union Champion, Richie Sandoval. It was an impressive line-up of boxing celebrities at a bargain price, only $2 at the door. This was another major success for the Crown City Boxing Stables, as well as for the Black Student Union, who earned additional revenue by running their own concession stand. Canto donated all his share of the collected funds to the school club.

◈◈

I stayed in close communication with my parents when I was in San Jose pursuing my teaching career. My mother informed me that my father was now taking Zanax medication for anxiety, was hearing voices from the past again, and was losing his appetite. He stopped going into the gym, and my mother feared that his psychological condition was declining. Canto complained about not being able to sleep well and had to be kept from doubling up on his medicines.

Canto fluctuated between the past and the present. He often wondered what happened to his old manager, Tom Donahue. When Canto's brothers dropped by to visit him and try to cheer him up, he seemed unresponsive. They invited him out to dinner but he refused. My uncles Manuel and Julio often visited with a gunny sack full of fish they had caught, since my mother had a tasty fish recipe that Canto loved. They hoped her special fish dishes would perk him up. But depression had set in, and it was harder and harder for our family to break through to Canto.

In the midst of these emerging concerns, I decided to leave my teaching assignment in San Jose, resigning at the end of the school year, and came home to help my parents, at least to take over gym obligations and relieve job pressures. I started training in the gym right away, helping my father with all the fighters. My mother felt bad that I was sacrificing my own career to my parents' needs, but I explained to her that helping them out was the most important thing to me. They had raised me well.

❧❧

Meeting My Future Wife

But things were changing for me, too. It was 1979, when I'd gone, after working in the gym, to my cousin Raymond Mercado's house to relax. He had invited me to come over to play some guitar with him. His wife Grace was also there, along with their son, Little Ray. Raymond and I were playing guitar in his living room when in walked the most beautiful girl I had ever seen.

This young lady was the sister of Raymond's wife, Grace. Her name was Josie, and what an attractive young lady she was! Josie had dropped by to borrow a sleeping bag because she was going on a camping trip with her older sister and her brother-in-law. Josie had long, wavy black hair and beautiful, captivating green eyes. I was in a trance, staring at her. She was in a hurry, with her family waiting in the car because they were on their way to Ensenada for the weekend. Raymond introduced Josie to me, and I uttered some platitudes awkwardly. Josie's engaging smile put me at ease, as did her gentle manner. I was smitten with her like I'd never felt before. She said her farewells and hurried out. Raymond and I continued playing music, but I couldn't get her off my mind. Later I asked Raymond if she was married or going out with anyone in particular. Was she dating someone? Raymond said she was single. My heart soared.

I continued to substitute teach for the Pasadena school district and work with my father's fighters in the gym. I decided to enroll at California State University in Los Angeles with the objective of receiving an Adapted Physical Education certificate, which would enable me to teach PE to children with special needs. On this new personal enhancement trajectory, I contacted Josie, asked her for a date, and we started dating regularly. I fell in love with her right away. All I knew was I wanted to marry her.

I talked about Josie with my parents, detailing how I felt about her.

My father said in a calm voice: "If you love her, my son, you should ask her to marry you."

"Yes, it's the best thing to do," agreed my mother.

I felt affirmed.

My mother added, "I'm very happy for you, happy that you've found someone to love and cherish the rest of your life." As always, her words were heartfelt.

I decided to propose to Josie and made reservations at La Fonda Mexican Restaurant in Los Angeles, which had a dinner show and entertainment. I invited Josie's parents, along with my parents and my Aunt Nora, to go to the dinner show with us. Josie had no idea that I was planning to propose to her, but happily, she agreed to marry me. We married the following year and began a new generation of the Robledo family.

❧❧

The gift of life is the most precious thing any of us have. It is the precariousness of life, though, that heightens its value to us. So, when Josie became pregnant, the expectation of a new life entering into our home was blissful and uplifting. We were thrilled at the prospect of another Robledo coming into the world, our very own little Robledo. The baby was due in January.

When the milestone day arrived, Josie began experiencing labor pains and, when it was time to take her to the hospital, I phoned my mother and father to let them know what was happening and what hospital to go to. When Josie and I arrived at the hospital door, she was having intense, accelerated labor pains and was taken to the delivery room. Her labor was very long and difficult for her. She finally gave birth to our first baby, but the baby's umbilical cord was wrapped around his neck, and he had other medical problems. Despite heroic efforts on the part of doctors and nurses, our baby, Julian Canto Robledo, died five days later.

৵৩৵৩

My father was contacted by TV Channel 7 Eyewitness News, which wanted to do a short documentary on him and his Boxing Stables. He invited studio management to come by the Stables, or to send their production crew, and they could experience the gym firsthand while they filmed on location. This would give welcome visibility to our gym and would hopefully attract more boxers. The news team agreed to film onsite and went to the Boxing Stables to film the fighters working out and to interview Canto. They held on to the tape for later release. They intended to film further at some of Canto's boxing events to catch him in action as he managed his boxers in the ring. They would film the Timmy Martinez bout later.

Soon after this documentary, Canto was approached by a magazine called *Q-VO*, which had political and social stories of the time. They also featured low-riding cars of the past, along with beautiful girls. A journalist called my father wanting a special interview with her about Canto's Boxing Stables. She wrote a very complimentary article that captured the spirit of my father's mission in his life's work. Our family was proud of this recognition of our father.

(See citation for this article, "Warrior of the Ring," November 1980, in Appendix A). Canto was 67 years old.

This was not the last of the articles that were written about Canto in his later years. Though his age was catching up to him, and he was slowing down, his devotion to his boxers and their development did not diminish with time.

⋘⋙

My Growing Family

I was now 30 years old, teaching as much as I could, and overseeing our family's gym. Canto and Concha were as active as possible in the community, but Canto spent more and more time with his wife, relaxing in the comfort of their home. We, Canto's immediate family, stayed close to him, with the understandable exception of my brother Bobby. He had been released from the state hospital he'd been in for five years and was living with our sister Irene. Bobby occasionally visited our parents, sometimes staying with them on the weekends. Bobby seemed much calmer in these years. He was not as agitated anymore and enjoyed relaxing at home with his favorite beverage, beer, every now and then.

In 1982, Josie and her mother went to Josie's prenatal exam in Los Angeles. The doctor determined that Josie's water bag was leaking, and they would have to induce labor. The doctor admitted her to the hospital, which was directly across the street. Josie drove herself and her mother over, and my wife stayed overnight.

Early next morning, I drove to the hospital to see how Josie was progressing. The doctor induced labor, and after several hours of labor pains, our baby daughter, our eldest child, was born. It had been a difficult, hard labor. Our baby had a touch of yellow jaundice, but otherwise she was healthy and strong. We had not decided what to name our baby. Josie wanted the name Erica, and I wanted Jolene. We wrote each name on a separate piece of paper and placed both slips in a basket, which I shook a bit before Josie drew a slip. The name was Erica. We were both ecstatic when we were able to bring Erica Jolene

Robledo home with us to Alhambra. Later, we moved to Grand Oaks Street in Pasadena to be closer to Canto and the rest of our family.

৶৶

When I had first come home from San Jose to help my father in the gym, one of my first trainees was a young man named Timmy Martinez. He was a professional boxer with six fights and an average record to his name. I was impressed with Timmy not only because of his commitment to his sport, but also because of his commitment to his family. I learned soon after my arrival that Timmy had full custody of his two young children and he was working eight hours a day and boxing at night to support his family. I gave Timmy my best efforts, realizing that the sacrifice he was making went beyond the normal.

My father had scheduled Timmy to fight at the Olympic Auditorium. Channel 7 Eyewitness News had already filmed at the stables but had not aired the documentary and now wanted to film the bout. Canto told them they were more than welcome to do so.

Timmy was scheduled to fight a six-rounder against Sal Ramirez. The film crew followed us from the dressing room to the ring. They filmed my dad in the corner and between the rounds as a second in the corner. Timmy fought adequately well in the first round and survived the second round, but in the third round, he was caught with a left-right combination that staggered him. The referee called the fight off. My father was furious. He felt Timmy could have recovered well enough to finish the round to stay in the fight. The referee had not given him a standing eight count. He had simply waved his arms signaling the end of the contest. I agreed with my father: the referee should not have ended the fight so soon.

৶৶

In my own little family, Josie was pregnant again, and we were excited about our second child, due that August, my own birth month. I wondered if the baby would be a boy. If so, would he continue the Robledo boxing legacy? Josie had a good pregnancy this time around, feeling strong and healthy. When the time for the baby's birth arrived, Josie went into labor early in the morning, had a smooth delivery, and presented me with a healthy boy whom we named Phillip. It was a very joyous occasion for the large Jimenez and Robledo families, who were thankful for the safe arrival of this child. They were all happy that we had a girl and a boy.

CHAPTER 19:
The Professional Game of Boxing

The 1980's continued being a time of change and reinvention, not just for my little growing family, but for Canto and his Boxing Stables as well. Some of these involved my attaining my own professional certification as a boxing trainer and manager, which enabled me to help my father in more meaningful ways. In addition, our best fighters at Crown City Boxing Stables were increasingly competitive and were garnering the attention that earned them matchups with highly ranked boxers, or boxers who had fought very highly ranked fighters, such as Muhammad Ali. One such boxer from Canto's stables who was rising quickly in his career was a Pasadena local boy named Joey Olivera.

❦❦

Joey Olivera in Canto's Gym

In the early 1980's, teenagers Joey Olivera and his good friend, José Luis Correa, were training at the gym. The boys were about 13 or 14 years old. Joey Olivera had been introduced to the Crown City Boxing Stables by José Luis, who had already been working out with Canto for a while. Both boys played on the football team at Pasadena High School. Joey wanted to get in better shape for the team, and he also wanted to know more about boxing after watching it on television. Plus, he had seen the movie "Rocky", which inspired him to box.

Before José Luis took Joey to meet Canto, he had told him: "There's just one catch. Canto is blind."

Joey had been surprised. "Blind? Then how does he train the boxers?"

"Who am I to question a 65-year-old man?" said Jose. "He charges $10 dollars a month to work out. He will also give you boxing lessons."

This fascinated Olivera, and he wanted to know more about Canto, so he decided to go visit his gym on Manzanita Street.

Joey was coached at Pasadena High School by Coach Braxton, as he was called by everyone. Coach knew Canto and his community work very well. He allowed Joey to do his fitness training at Canto's gym, then report to the football field after he was done. Joey showed up faithfully, covered in sweat. All the coaches for the team knew of Canto and his Boxing Stables. They were supportive of Joey's boxing dreams. Also, according to Joey's mother, Joey was being recruited by local gangs, and she feared that he might fall prey to negative, dangerous influences. This was additional motivation for Canto to inspire Joey to stick with boxing.

After a few months of training Joey, Canto decided it was time for him to have his first amateur bout in Azusa, a nearby city. Joey had been sparring with his friend Correa, and Canto felt Joey was ready. The debut bout was scheduled for three rounds with a one-minute rest between rounds and was held at the Saint Francis Parish Hall patio. Joey fought solidly but did not have the experience needed to win. He finished the rounds strong but lost on a decision to his opponent, who was from Azusa. Neither Joey nor Canto diminished their conviction that Joey had talent and could accomplish a lot.

My father and Joey developed a special bond. Canto treated him like a son and enjoyed training him in the gym. Canto made sure Joey was doing his road work and staying out of the streets. He did not want him in any gangs. Joey followed his directions and guidance.

Canto called him almost every night after 10 p.m. to make sure he was at home. He expected Joey in the gym six days a week and running seven days. Canto knew that Joey was driven to become the best fighter in his division. He trained very hard and was a self-starter. Canto never had to tell him to get ready. Joey was very punctual in arriving at the gym and was usually the last to leave. Joey was solicitous and helpful toward Canto outside of the gym as well, driving my father around to various boxing matches in other gyms. My father taught Joey what it takes to accomplish the goal of being a champion. He taught Joey that champions are not ordinary people.

Olivera once said: "I wanted people to recognize Canto, just as I wanted recognition myself."

In 1983, Canto signed Joey Olivera to a five-year pro contract with me being his primary trainer. This was an honor for me, and I felt grateful to my father that he had inspired and positioned me for such work. Overall, this was a very busy time for me in the gym. I was training Jon Michael Roy, José Luis Correa, and Alonzo Hidalgo in addition to Joey. We had some serious prospects in the gym, and my father was determined to get a champion out of this group of fighters.

Not long after this, Joey got his pro debut match. Bill Kaplan, from the Casa Camino Real Club in Reseda, California, wanted to match Joey Olivera in a four-round match against Thomas Rodriguez, who was also making his pro debut. Olivera won a unanimous decision over Rodriguez. Bill Kaplan gave Joey the name of the "The Pasadena Kid," and Joey was on his way to bigger things.

❧❧

Leon Smith: Brief Glory

One evening while I worked out the fighters in the stables, a new African American boxer walked through the door. He had a wide smile and looked to be in shape. He was from Virginia, he said, and his name was Leon Smith. He claimed that he had over 80 amateur bouts to his name and had won a couple of state amateur titles back home. My father, who was sitting on the rub down table, spoke to him and introduced me to him. Leon wanted to start a professional boxing career in California. He had heard about Canto from a few local relatives.

Canto asked Leon, "How much do you weigh?"

"I weigh 135 pounds," Leon replied.

My father asked, "Do you have any workout gear with you?"

"Yes, sir. It's in the car," said Leon.

Canto told him, "Go get your things, come back, and train with us for a while, then we'll talk."

Leon shadow boxed a few rounds, and I could tell he understood the fundamentals of boxing. He had a superior left jab and a solid left hook. He could hit the double-end bag well, and the speed ball was easy for him to hit.

My father asked me to take him on the focus pads, which I did for four rounds. Leon moved well and knew how to block punches. He had clearly been taught how to jab and throw the one-two left hook combination. He had outstanding footwork and balance. Canto wasn't satisfied, though, and wanted to see Leon spar with Timmy Martinez. They sparred three rounds, and Leon worked well. Timmy came after him, but Leon was clever and held his own against a professional fighter. Clearly, he had experience and was ready to fight professionally. I told my father that Leon was a "made fighter," a boxer who was ready to compete.

"Let's sign him to a contract right away and get him a fight at the Olympic as soon as possible," I suggested to Canto.

This was done, and Leon had a great start out of the gate. He won several fights in a row, displaying impressive boxing skills. The management from the Silver Slipper Casino in Las Vegas, Nevada, wanted to use Leon to fight an upcoming star from Ohio. His name was Ray "Boom Boom" Mancini. My father booked the fight, and Leon fought a 10-round bout with Mancini. Unfortunately, Leon was over-matched, and Mancini knocked him out in the first round.

Shortly afterward, Leon and Canto accepted another fight in Bakersfield, California, where Leon was matched against a tough fighter by the name of Gonzalo Montellano. This contest was scheduled for 10 rounds, and Leon hurt Gonzalo many times throughout the fight. The judges had favored Gonzalo, the hometown favorite, and gave him a split decision win.

After the contest was over, we had to go see Harry Kabakoff, the promoter of the show, to get paid. I led my father to the hotel room, and Harry was waiting for us with a stack of bills. He was paying us in cash. I could see he had a loaded revolver on the bed next to the cash and his briefcase. He liked my father very much and told him that Leon had won the fight, but the hometown judges gave the verdict to Gonzalo out of bias.

A few months later, Canto was offered a 6-round matchup for Leon, an opponent named Carlton Sparrow from Las Vegas. Sparrow was 18-0. Transportation and lodging were always included along with the fight fee. My father loved going to Las Vegas and truly enjoyed playing the slot machines. Canto enjoyed the sound of coins dropping into the tray and kept excellent track of his winnings. He put the coins in a small bucket and was able to distinguish the differences in size among the various coins. This is how he was able to determine the amount of his winnings. When it came to the bills, he placed his singles first, then the fives, tens, twenties and so on, and gave each bill a slightly different corner fold on the edge to distinguish their face values. He also had me count his money and help him keep track of it for him. He had always loved Las Vegas and was eager to go for this match.

I conducted some research on Carlton Sparrow and was dismayed to learn how formidable he was. He had 12 KO's and was undefeated. He was a right-handed fighter with tremendous knockout power with both hands and with an extensive amateur record. I had been noticing in the gym that Leon was losing his dedication and hunger to be the best in the game. I had observed his reflexes slowing down. He didn't practice very long in the gym anymore. His conditioning was also suspect. He skipped out on training runs with Olivera and Correa. I would often drive him down to the bridle path at the Rose Bowl to run, but he frequently refused and said he had somewhere else to go.

While training Leon, I was able to hit him with the focus pads with some good left hooks and right crosses that he should have been able to block. After getting hit on the chin, he'd laugh and say, "Good shot, Joe!" I told my father all these facts and my opinion that this would not be a good fight for Leon. This Sparrow fighter was too good for Leon. I also told my father that our Leon now was not the same Leon who had walked into the gym a year ago.

But Leon pleaded with Canto to let him take this fight, so that he would be able to buy a plane ticket back to Virginia. He was very homesick at the time. He assured Canto that he would train harder and get in better shape and be ready for the fight. Sadly, Leon was knocked out in the fourth round.

❧❧

Navigating the Trainers' World

I never took for granted my great fortune in being Canto Robledo's son. I know that this alone was not sufficient for success in my new side job of being a certified trainer and manager, but I still valued the headstart that my father had given me in learning the fundamentals of the boxing game and being able to know the administrative players of the profession. I was fortunate enough to get on the inside of the boxing world quickly. I began to meet various trainers and managers, such as Angelo Dundee, Johnny Flores, Jackie McCoy, Thell Torrance, Duke Holloway, Dubs from the Main Street Gym, Memo Santo from Hawthorne, Norman Lockwood, and many others.

Norman Lockwood managed and controlled the dungeon-like dressing rooms at the Olympic Auditorium. Everyone needed permission from him to enter the actual dressing rooms, and they all had to have credentials, so access was limited to those working on the card as a corner man or with a fighter. Norman had a list of names on a clipboard who were allowed in. He was a very strict man, but if he liked you, he helped you.

He truly enjoyed being around Canto in the dressing rooms and was a key advisor to Canto and me. He sat and talked with Canto about up-and-coming fighters, as well as reminisce about the past. Not everyone got close to Norman, but it was obvious that he and my father had a friendly relationship. As a result, I was in with Norman, who knew I was Canto's son, and Norman would give me tips on the fights. He was kind and generous with us, often giving us the used boxing gloves in a brown paper bag at the end of the boxing shows. He knew we had many fighters in our gym who needed gear.

Norman allowed me to watch the hands of fighters being wrapped. The dressing rooms were quite small to begin with, so only a selected few men could watch the wrapping of the hands. Certain trainers didn't mind us watching, but other trainers would not allow us to watch. I loved it! I watched, enraptured, and observed closely how each trainer had his own special way of hand-wrapping.

≈≈≈

Jon Michael Roy

In 1985, the ESPN Sports Network's Middleweight Championship Tournament was underway, and they needed a last-minute replacement. The fighter who was scheduled to fight was sick in the hospital, so the network needed a substitute to fill the main event card. The matchmaker had noticed one of my boxers, Jon Michael Roy, in San Jose, California, was sufficiently impressed with him, and figured that he would be a good match for Alberto Gonzalez. Gonzalez was the favorite to win the entire championship, but I agreed to the matchup.

Jon Michael Roy fought like there was no tomorrow. He was a steady aggressor with a vicious body attack on Gonzalez. He had him hurt several times throughout the contest. Roy was the split decision winner that night and advanced in the tournament. He was scheduled to fight Lee Sanders in January at the Caesars Tahoe Stateline, Nevada. Roy defeated Sanders in a unanimous decision and now advanced to the championship title fight in Las Vegas scheduled for February.

On the day before the fight, I was unable to fly with Roy to Las Vegas, to prep for the match, as is usual for trainers/managers to do. I had my teaching obligations. My supervisors, our school administrators, had called me into the office shortly before the fight and informed me that they would not approve my leaving class for two days. The principal was displeased with me for the many days I'd missed teaching because I was at boxing matches instead. He had seen me on television and told me that I had to make up my mind as to what profession I would commit myself. I had been leaving my students for several days with a substitute teacher. I told him that I would be more dedicated henceforth to the children and my professional obligations to the school. I had known prior to this ultimatum from my principal that I would have to make serious decisions regarding teaching versus training. I was making very good supplemental money with the fight game.

For now, I had this immediate fight to attend. It was scheduled at the Showboat Hotel & Casino in Las Vegas. This was a 10-round bout for the tournament championship and a new 1985 Chrysler to go with the prize. The purse was more than Michael Roy had ever earned from boxing. His opponent was Charles Campbell from Louisiana. After teaching that Friday, I flew up immediately to be with Michael at the Showboat Hotel Casino for the fight that night.

When I met Jon Michael Roy in his room, it was obvious he had been partying the night before. I was shocked and upset. I reinforced to him the huge significance of this fight. He assured me that things would work out fine, not to worry. Once the fight commenced, however, Michael looked anything but fine. In the first round, his legs were rubbery and unbalanced, and his jab was slow and ineffective, with little head movement. Campbell was able to land a solid combination on Michael's chin, and down he went for an eight-count. He got himself up but his eyes were bleary. The barrage of punches continued till the bell saved him.

When he came and sat in the corner, I told him to use his jab followed by a three-part combination and to hit Campbell hard with the right hand. But, at the bell, Campbell attacked Roy with a vengeance again and quickly dropped him for a ten-count. The fight was over. Roy was ingloriously knocked out in the second round of the championship fight.

❧❧

Canto had been contacted by Churchill Films for a documentary they wanted to produce using Canto and his Crown City Boxing Stables. This would be a one-hour prime-time KCOP special featuring Canto and Joey Olivera working out and preparing for an upcoming fight at the Olympic Auditorium. They filmed Joey doing his road work on Pasadena streets. The film was a large production with cameras, lights, and plenty of action. I enjoyed helping as much as possible, since most of the filming occurred in the gym.

Churchill Films, responsible for the entire content of the documentary, called "Down for the Count," took a position that boxing was a brutal, outdated sport that should be banned. They featured my father in a negative way. The film depicted Canto as a victim of the sport. Very little was dedicated to his charitable work with the youth of Pasadena. The publicity brochure for the film included this blurb: "[This] is a compelling and thought- provoking inside view of the fighters, matchmakers and the bureaucracy that pit possible injury and death against the elusive promise of fame and wealth for those who make it to the big time."

They also featured various fighters commenting on boxing, such as Muhammad Ali, Art Aragon, and Larry Holmes. I personally met all three of these top boxers at the time of filming. We watched Ali work out in Santa Monica, California. My father was reunited with his old friend Art Aragon. They had a great time together remembering fighters of the past.

The film was nominated for an Emmy Award in the short documentary category. We were invited to attend the screening in Hollywood. After the screening, I was deeply disappointed with the content of the film. We had no control over the final cut of the film, and I told the director that I felt the film was a biased statement against boxing, and I didn't like the way they portrayed my father. I received a letter a few days later from film officials with the following remark: "'Down for the Count' pulls no punches. It is an uncompromising one-hour look at a sport that may not survive in its present form by the end of this century." They even had a quote from an American Medical Association member: "There is no doubt in my mind that boxing should be banned. It's less of a sport than a cockfight. It has no place in civilized society."

This, of course, was before cage fighting became popular and before the MMA fight game became wildly popular. I wonder what the producer of "Down for the Count" thought about boxing after seeing the popularity of these other sports.

⚜⚜

Tragedy Strikes the Crown City Boxing Stables

My cousin Raymond Mercado often visited the gym, watching the fighters work out, and helping in the gym whenever he could. He liked to help with the amateur boxers, holding the heavy bag while they worked out on it. After observing Raymond's work in the gym for several weeks, I told my father that Raymond was learning to train fighters quickly and could be an asset to the stables. This would also help me with my training load. My father decided to train Raymond on the proper techniques of boxing, including the focus pads.

At this time, in the late 1980's, Raymond was helping a new amateur prospect, Kingsley "Bam Bam" Brock. He was 14 years old, weighed 160 pounds, and stood 6 feet tall. He was very big and strong for his age and had been coming to the gym for about two years now. He wanted to be a professional fighter and cherished Canto's guidance in his amateur career. Kingsley's mother had asked Canto to keep her son in the gym and off the streets, where the gang- bangers were constantly trying to recruit him. Canto had taken a liking to this new prospect and wanted to help him as much as possible.

Canto monitored Brock's activities like a father, checking on him whenever he wasn't in the gym, encouraging him to follow his dreams of being a professional boxer. Canto saw great talent and potential in Brock, who had won championships already at his young age. But one night, all this promise came to a resounding crash.

Our gym received the news that Bam Bam Brock had been murdered the night before, that he had been found in a car. It seemed that the gang culture had caught up with him. Canto had booked the young man to fight at the Olympic Auditorium for the National Junior Golden Gloves Championship, Middleweight Division. But now his mother, our gym, and our community had suddenly, tragically lost this rising star. It was a difficult time for us all.

Joey's Continuing Success

Joey Olivera had been winning big his last two fights and was making front-page news. He was now working out in a gym next to the Olympic Auditorium operated by Jim Gilio, who had matchmaking connections with a Hawaiian promoter. Jim was interested in booking a fight in Honolulu for Joey against the number one challenger from the Oriental Boxing Association who was also the state champion of Hawaii. His name was Rod Sequin, from Honolulu.

It would be a 10-round affair with all transportation and lodging included. We would stay 5 days. The fight weight limit was 135 pounds. This sounded very good. I talked it over with Canto and Joey, who were in favor of booking the fight. Canto considered Joey a very seasoned fighter with good experience and a winning streak. All this would put him in good stead for such a fight.

I called Jim and accepted his offer. Joey and I would fly to Honolulu to fight on a main event card at the Blaisdell Arena. I was very excited about this match. I knew Joey was in top shape ready for all comers. The match maker called us and said that Rod Sequin was ill and had to pull out of the fight, but they now had a replacement, a fighter from South Korea. His name was Oh Kyu Chang, the number one contender from the Oriental Boxing Federation (OBF). This was a surprise for Joey and me, but we had to take the fight, since the Blaisdell Arena was sold out for the 10-round contest.

We were invited to a press conference the day before the fight with the promoters and press. Sitting in the room was Chang, who was with his trainer and interpreter. Several questions were asked of both fighters, and Chang remarked that he had trouble with southpaws, which in the boxing world is a fighter who jabs with his right hand instead of the typical left-handed jab. Joey and I looked at each other and realized Chang had given us an opportunity to exploit his weakness. Joey started the fight as a southpaw, which made a big difference in the outcome of the contest.

Chang was a dirty fighter in the ring, attacking with his elbows and head to try and slow Joey's assault. It didn't work. Joey knocked down Chang several times. In the tenth round, near the end of the fight, Chang head-butted Joey, inflicting a deep cut on the left eyebrow. When the bell sounded for the end of the fight, Chang knew he had lost and left the ring before the decision was rendered. He never congratulated Joey on the fight. He was a dejected, poor loser. (See citation to article, "Olivera defeats Chang in Hawaii," March 1986, in Appendix A.)

Some time afterward, Canto and I heard that the Fabulous Forum in Inglewood, California was going to stage the Stroh's Beer Lightweight Tournament. We personally knew Tony Curtis, the matchmaker, who was in charge of producing the tournament. I asked him about entering Joey in this prestigious contest and was told by management that Joey hadn't fought enough quality fighters and didn't own any state titles. I lobbied for Joey until Curtis relented and told Canto and me that he would have Joey fight Felipe Sanchez from Mexico, who had a very good ring record. If Joey could defeat Sanchez in a 10-round contest, he would qualify for the tournament. All he had to do was win big in grand style with an early knockout.

Raymond and I worked Joey out very hard for this fight. We had him in tip-top condition with plenty of quality sparring. I had the chance to see Sanchez work out in Los Angeles and could thus prepare Joey more strategically. Sanchez was a fighter who liked to counterpunch and seemed to be in good condition. His movements were similar to Joey's: he liked to come in close and mix it up while counter-punching. The bout was hard-fought, with Joey stopping Sanchez in the third round, a very impressive win. Joey was subsequently invited to participate in the Stroh's Beer Boxing Tournament.

Tony Curtis informed us that Joey would be fighting against John Sinegal from Texas, who was ranked #4 in the tournament by the Southern Boxing Association. The bout was scheduled for August 13, 1986. Finally we had our big chance to win the grand prize of $50,000. But first Joey had to win four straight fights in the tournament to capture this title. He was the underdog. Canto and I felt that the promoters really did not want Joey in there mixing things up. He was a spoiler and most likely was not on the promoters' short list of favorites. Their preferences didn't matter, though: Joey won that match by knocking out Sinegal in the fifth round with a vicious body attack. This victory was a big one for Canto's Crown City Boxing Stables. Joey was putting us on the map.

We stayed focused on moving forward. Next up was the highly talented Freddie Pendleton from Florida. Pendleton was favored to win the tournament and capture the title. All bets were on Pendleton to knock Joey out in the fight. But, once more, those in the know really didn't know Joey and his immense grit. He fought his heart out for 10 impressive rounds. Going into the last round, Pendleton must have known he was behind in the score cards, so he pulled a dirty trick, thumbing Joey in the left eye. The fight was momentarily stopped so Joey could be checked out by the ringside doctor. He was given the okay to continue, and Pendleton swarmed all over Olivera, but the bell sounded, and the fight was over. Joey won by a decision. He had just upset the favorite!

Team Robledo stayed focused, not taking anything for granted. Next in Joey Olivera's path to the finals was a showdown with Walter Sims. Joey and Walter had fought against each other in the past, with Joey losing both times to Sims. This was a highly anticipated rematch, with the winner advancing into the championship round and a chance to win the $50,000 prize. (See citation for the article, "Semi-Final Showdown with Walter Sims," by the *Los Angeles Times* Staff writer, Steve Springer, December 1986 in Appendix A).

In the 10-round semi-final match, Joey controlled Sims for 6 rounds and hurt Sims several times in the fight. Joey moved from side to side, connecting with vicious combinations off Sims' face. Walter Sims looked weak, awkward, and off-balance. Joey had staggered him a few times and was in total control until the seventh round, when Joey decided to switch to a southpaw position in the latter rounds. Unfortunately, this seemed to energize Sims, and he mounted an aggressive comeback. The fight ended up being closer than it was on the scorecard. It was a decision for Walter Sims.

When Sims was announced as the winner, the Forum crowd booed the decision loudly. Even the sportscasters felt Joey had pulled off another upset. I felt they had robbed us of victory. Canto was so upset, he kicked the water bucket across the ring, and it landed in the judges' laps. The irony was not lost on many observers: a sightless man kicked a bucket perfectly, purposely or not, at the target of his ire, whereas the sighted judges had missed the target of a justified decision. Still, this kicking of the bucket carried consequences. As the chief second trainer in Joey's corner, I had to pay a fine to the boxing commission. (See citation for article in the *Los Angeles Times*, "Sims

Reaches Lightweight Final with a Unanimous Decision over Olivera," December 1986.)

෯෯

More Attention from the Media

Canto had been contacted by the great Jim Murray, a distinguished sportswriter for the *Los Angeles Times*. He wanted to write a story about Canto and his sightless world and how Canto had managed his successful life all these years. Jim was losing his eyesight in one eye and wondered how Canto was able to navigate life in a darkened world. He visited my father at his home in Pasadena. Murray also interviewed my mother at length, for she had been Canto's eyes for so many years, for most of his life, in fact. Murray also interviewed me about my father's condition and how we did our work at the Stables. At the end of the interview, Murray asked Canto if he had any regrets, and what would he do over? Without skipping a beat, Canto replied: "I have no regrets, but if I had to do it over again, well, I would have ducked more." (See citation for the article, "Fall in Line," July 1986 in Appendix A.)

Our family also started getting calls from various TV networks wanting to interview Canto and Joey Olivera. Journalists from Channel 13 KCOP, from Hollywood, were intrigued by this blind manager and trainer of professional fighters. They came to our gym and filmed Canto training his boxers. They were so impressed with his skills and abilities, that they named Canto "Sports Star of the Month." They gave him a special T-shirt with their TV logo on the front and, more important, two seats to a Clippers basketball game. At the end of the interview with Rich Chambers, while the cameras were still rolling, my father took the shirt, felt it with his hands, and told the commentator, "This shirt feels cheap to me." It was all set up as a joke, and it came off very funny. The film was aired a few days later on Channel 13, KCOP.

෯෯

Joey Olivera's Title Fight

In 1987, Canto received a phone call from promoter Don Fraser, who wanted to schedule Joey in a USA California State Title fight against Larry Villarreal from Fresno. The fight would be a 12-round main event held under the wing of the world-famous mammoth airplane built by billionaire Howard Hughes, the Spruce Goose. Permanently stationed in Long Beach, California, the gigantic plane has been an international tourist attraction for many decades. The choice of this location would undoubtedly attract much interest not just locally, but across the nation and beyond.

The fight was scheduled for February 9, 1987 and would be shown on local TV channels. This was an immense boost for Canto's stables and a great opportunity for Joey to win his first USA California State Lightweight Title. Team Robledo had to get Joey in top shape with plenty of intensive sparring. Raymond, our trainer and family member, was instrumental in training Joey, insuring that Joey was doing his road work around the Rose Bowl and at the popular Pasadena High School track.

The title fight was an exciting show of nonstop action beneath the Spruce Goose. Larry Villarreal seemed more aggressive than Joey in this fight. Joey lacked that killer instinct that a champion must possess to win a title. Early in the rounds, Villarreal connected more frequently and with sharper, more accurate punches. Joey was off-balance that night and never seemed to recover. Villarreal won by a unanimous decision.

We were all very dejected with the outcome and with Joey's fight plan. He was lacking something, and it was not conditioning. Joey lacked the desire and willpower to overtake Villarreal. Canto told Joey to take some time off and rest before coming back to the gym. He wanted Joey to really think about his boxing future and what he wanted to do. Joey had to figure things out for himself at this point in his career. Joey ended up taking 8-10 weeks off from training in the gym.

Don Fraser contacted Canto again about scheduling another state title shot between Joey and the new state champion, Ernie

Landeros. The fight would be a 12-rounder, again under the wing of the Spruce Goose. Landeros had defeated Larry Villarreal earlier in the year and had taken his title. Landeros was willing to defend it against Joey Olivera, "the Pasadena Kid." A few years ago, Ernie and Joey had fought in the Golden Gloves Tournament on two occasions, splitting the two fights with decisions. Landeros had a grudge against Joey for some odd reason. He was from Eagle Rock, California, a small city next to Pasadena, so it may have been a case of hometown rivalries.

I knew that Ernie Landeros would be a tough and challenging opponent. He was a stocky fighter with a big upper body and short, powerful arms. He crowded his opponents, didn't use much movement, but dealt heavy right and left hooks. He was always in superb condition and came ready to fight. I had seen Ernie fight as an amateur and professional and knew he was a very formidable opponent. I did not know that Ernie had been in a serious car accident several months earlier. I found out later after the fight. However, the State Athletic Boxing Commission's doctor had cleared him to fight, so the fight was set. Ernie was a gutsy fighter with tremendous power in both hands who was determined to hold onto his state title.

As it turned out, the judges had Joey behind in the fight when it was stopped, because Landeros was unable to continue the fight, due to cuts over his eyes and the right side of his head. Joey busted him up pretty well in the fight. The judges gave the win to Joey. We finally caught a decision that went our way.

My father and mother were highly pleased and thankful that we brought a state title, State of California Lightweight Championship, home to the Crown City Boxing Stables. Joey "the Pasadena Kid" Olivera had helped us add this championship jewel on the "crown" of the stables!

<img ❧❧

New Show, New Baby

Shortly after the fight, my father was contacted by Channel 4 KNBC from Hollywood. They had a new series called "Real People." It was a show that showcased individuals performing real and unusual activities. My father was asked to be on the show. They wanted to come to the gym and film Canto training the boxers. It went very well for Canto and the stables. The television program was aired on national television and this was very exciting for Canto and our family.

There were more good happenings for the Robledo family in the spring of 1987. Josie was expecting our third child. Just as the morning sun began to rise, she was scheduled to report to the hospital to undergo induced labor because the baby was one week overdue. Josie's parents came to our house to take care of Erica and Phillip while we were at the hospital. Not everything went smoothly, and there were moments during which the doctor was concerned. Our second son, Andrew, was born with some medical complications and was immediately taken to the neo-natal ward for close monitoring. We found out that Andrew had been born with special needs. He was kept in the hospital for about 10 days, then was released to come home. We were all excited to finally have him home with us. It was truly a joyous occasion, with my little family now complete. Andrew is now 31 years old and doing well.

CHAPTER 20:
Canto's Championship Belt, At Last

We wanted to strike while the iron was hot, as the old cliché goes. In December we arranged a bout for Joey in Las Vegas at the Bally's Hotel and Casino. We scheduled the fight for January 8, 1988. The fight would be against highly ranked Chris Calvin, the fighting rebel from the South. He was also a rising main event fighter who wanted to box for the world's title. His ring record was 21-5-2. Calvin fought mostly on the East Coast, and ESPN was backing him in this fight. Al Bernstein was the fight commentator and analyst.

Shortly before we hit the road, my father had doubts about going on this trip. On the way to Las Vegas, he told us he didn't feel well and said we might have to take him back home. With us on this trip were Raymond Mercado, our corner man, and Forrest Morgan, a friend of my father's. Ray and Forrest would be able to assist with my father if needed. My father was nervous and uncomfortable; he really wanted to go home.

We arrived in Las Vegas at the hotel in the early afternoon. The weigh-in was scheduled for two o' clock. It was during the official weigh-in that Canto told me he still wasn't feeling well and wanted to go home. I called the doctor to check my dad out at ringside. His blood pressure was okay, and he had no temperature. The doctor told me it was a form of exhaustion, and he needed to rest. The continuing pressure of thinking about the upcoming fight made my father feel even more anxious. He told me again he wanted to go home, but I couldn't take him because the fight was scheduled that night, so my father agreed to be driven home by Forrest, who would return to Las Vegas alone immediately. My father wished Joey Olivera good luck and assured him that he'd win tonight. When my dad left, I felt that he was beginning to show signs of depression again.

As I was getting ready to start wrapping Joey's hands for the fight, a familiar, sharply-dressed boxer walked in to say good luck and hello to Joey. It was Sugar Ray Leonard, one of the all-time greatest welterweight champions in boxing history. He was very pleasant and cordial with us in his brief visit. Following the weigh-in, Joey, Raymond and I went upstairs to relax in our rooms. About three o' clock, we went to the hotel restaurant to have a light meal. After eating, we returned to Joey's room. Later that afternoon we had a scheduled interview with Al Bernstein, the boxing analyst and sportscaster for ESPN.

The fight was an exciting 10-round event that had everyone on the edge of their seats. Joey took control of Chris Calvin from the outset and was able to strike him at will. Joey was landing a three-part combination all night long, which seemed to confuse Calvin. Although Joey started to slow down in the ninth and tenth rounds, and Calvin came on strong, it was a little too late. Joey won on a split decision.

The following month, Joey was booked to fight the highly regarded Mickey Ward in a 10-round lightweight bout at Bally's Hotel and Casino in Las Vegas. Canto was still not feeling totally well and was thus unable to attend this fight. Joey was in good shape, but I felt we had needed two more weeks off from training to give Joey ample time to recover fully from the Calvin fight before going against a class "A" fighter like Ward. We were stepping up in class and these were the fighters now that Joey had to face and defeat in order to earn big money and a shot at the world title. Naturally, Joey would be the underdog.

Ward was a superb fighter with all the tools to be a world champion. His record at that time was 15-1-0. The house money was on Ward to knock out Joey within 5 rounds. Joey did his best and managed to give the audience a good fight, but he lacked the experience that Ward had. Ward could move and exchange punches with the best, and he wasn't afraid to mix it up with Joey. He wanted to take Joey out early, but Joey had other plans. It was an exciting 10 rounds of nonstop action. Joey was never hurt in the fight and tried his hardest to win. Ward was a better fighter that night, however, and won a unanimous decision.

More Recognition for Canto

A clerk from the office of Los Angeles Supervisor Michael Antonovich called our house one day and wanted to speak with Canto about a special award they wanted to present him in the Supervisor's office. They wanted to honor Canto for his career as a boxer and boxing coach for over 55 years. They had a beautiful scroll they had made especially for him. It was a touching tribute to him, and our family felt very proud of Canto. Inscribed on the scroll was the following:

> *[Canto Robledo] was also a world class bantam weight boxer, and the Pacific Coast Bantam Weight Champion. Despite an injury sustained during a bout which caused him to lose sight in both eyes, he has been coaching young fighters, training numerous boxers to world-class status, and has been spotlighted on numerous television shows, talk shows, magazine, and newspaper articles.*
>
> *The County of Los Angeles praises him for his devotion for more than 50 years in helping young men to leave gangs and get into a healthy sport and has worked for the United Way for Juvenile Diversion and the rewards of healthy competition.*
>
> *Let it be written that the Board of Supervisors commends Canto Robledo for his untiring efforts in the training and discipline of young boxers and for furthering the sport of boxing, especially to our youth.*

I remember this day well. My parents, my sisters, Gloria and Irene, and Joey drove to City Hall in Los Angeles to receive the award. We were escorted into the chambers of Supervisor Antonovich. After a short period, Antonovich came out to meet us and said a few words to my dad, congratulating him on this award. Canto and the rest of us took pictures together and had lunch in the City Hall Cafeteria. This was such a happy day for my father! My mother was ecstatic, and we all beamed with pride.

A few weeks later, my father was contacted by TV Channel 2 KNX regarding a television interview with Canto and Ken Norton. This was a talk show, question-and-answer format, called "Two with

You." My father was up for the show and really wanted to be part of the program. He was more than excited when we arrived at the Hollywood studios. Ken and my dad hit it off quite well. He had heard of Canto and wanted to talk with him about his fights with Speedy Dado, Midget Wolgast, and Young Sport. I was in the room as they both reminisced about their fights from the past. Ken was a nice, respectful, classy man, never arrogant, who made us feel totally comfortable around him.

The actual TV interview had each champion discussing his fights. My father spoke about how times were much different in the old days. He talked about having to fight at least three to four times a month to make enough money to feed his family. Norton, on the other hand, reminisced about his big fights with Muhammad Ali and Wayne Kindred. At the end of the show, we were escorted to a dining area where we had a beautiful and plentiful lunch together. The program aired a couple of weeks later. Our large family sat around the living room TV and tremendously enjoyed the show.

World Boxing Hall of Fame

A few days later, I received a phone call from Charles Casas, the president of the World Boxing Hall of Fame, who wanted to know more about Canto and his boxing, training, and managing career. I answered his questions, and he asked me if my family still had possession of Canto's Pacific Coast Bantamweight Championship belt, which he had won in 1932 in San Francisco, CA. I told him no. I explained to him the circumstances of my father's last fight with Hilo Hernandez, his ensuing blindness, and how Canto had never received his Pacific Coast Bantamweight Championship belt.

Casas asked me if it would be okay to honor Canto and present him with a championship title belt at the Banquet of Champions, World Boxing Hall of Fame Ninth Annual Dinner and Presentation, to be held on October 29, 1988 at the Marriott Hotel in Los Angeles. Casas wanted to induct Canto as a humanitarian in the sport of boxing at this special event. He also told me they were going to commission Joey Olmos, the Chief Athletic Boxing Inspector of California at that time, to make the special belt for Canto. Olmos was known for his skillful crafting of boxing shoes, body protectors, headgears, and other essential boxing equipment. He would design Canto's special belt.

At the event in October, Olmos, who knew Canto well, spoke of his fights against Speedy Dado, Young Sport, and Midget Wolgast. Olmos respected Canto very much for his continuous work with the youth and fighting juvenile delinquency. Canto was surrounded by some of his boxing friends from the past, legendary fighters such as Gene Fulmer, Mushy Callahan, Ingmar Johansson, Willie Pastrano, Joey Maxim, Armando Ramos, Enrique Bolanos, Muhammad Ali, Joe Fraser, Art Aragon, Danny "Lil Red" Lopez, Paul Gonzalez, Carlos Palomino, Sean O'Grady, Dub Harris, Aileen Eaton, and many more.

My father and I were asked to go onto the stage and receive his championship belt, presented with great dignity by Charles Casas. My father said a few words and thanked the World Boxing Hall of Fame for this special honor and his Championship belt. He thanked his wife Concha for over 50 years of her devotion, everlasting love, and support. This was an incredible night. We all celebrated the evening together as a team from the Crown City Boxing Stables.

I was excited and very happy for the way things turned out that night. We were getting much closer to the top of the professional boxing world. I could see myself training and managing world champions. I was meeting major players in the boxing game. I began to wonder if I should abandon my teaching career and choose a fulltime boxing profession instead.

๛๛

Joey Olivera and Us

But our joy in this honor for my father turned out to be short-lived. We shortly thereafter received a letter from the State Athletic Boxing Commission reminding us that Joey Olivera needed an eye and physical examination to get his new boxing license for the State of California. This was a normal procedure. Joey had not been complaining of any physical problems or injuries, and he told me he would go on his own to take the test. All seemed normal at this point, and I continued to train the boxers in the gym.

A few days later, Joey received a letter from the State Athletic Boxing Commission stating that he had not passed the eye examination due to a torn retina in the right eye. Joey came to the Stables with the letter, so I could read the results for myself. My father, upon hearing these news, was deeply saddened and wondered what had happened. Remembering that my father had been unable to attend the boxing match in which Joey was injured, I explained to Canto how the injury to his eye had occurred.

The Commission's findings and decision were devastating to Joey, Canto, and me. The Boxing Commission also declared that Joey was no longer able to box in California. His boxing license would be suspended indefinitely. Basically, he was no longer able to fight or to defend his state title in California. This was a devastating blow to Joey and the stables. After all his hard work and tough fights, his career was over, and his chances to earn a world title were gone.

Joey and I decided to get a second opinion from another eye specialist. After waiting a week, Joey and I made our way to the doctor's office, and Joey went in alone for his examination. I waited nervously in the outer office. The doctor finally came out with Joey, who had a patch over his right eye. The doctor confirmed that Joey's boxing days were over. He had a slightly torn retina and needed surgery to repair it. Joey figured it had been Pendleton who thumbed him in his eye in their fight.

This was devastating and depressing news, especially since it opened up Canto's old memories of his own loss. It was particularly important for Canto that Joey get good medical treatment. He didn't want Joey to suffer losing his eyesight, even if it were only in one eye. Thankfully, Joey later underwent a successful operation that restored his vision in his right eye, but he still had to give up his title by way of medical disqualification. This was the end of an important chapter in Canto Robledo's life and in my own, as well as Joey's. We had tasted championship victory and now tasted loss on several fronts: healthy eyesight, a championship, and Joey's ascendant career.

We all had to make adjustments in the Stables without Joey. For quite some time after this, my father was depressed and refused to come out to train the fighters. I wondered if he would once again spiral into deep depression. I had spoken with him to reassure him Joey was going to be okay. Canto was fighting the demons again, and I was trying to be his shield. I continued to train the fighters in the gym and was hopeful we could get back to normal. We couldn't let hope die.

CHAPTER 21:
Eyes Darkened Once Again

On Friday, November 18, 1988, the day started out as a normal teaching day. I called my mother as I usually did to inquire about my father. She told me he was feeling better and was in the gym hitting the heavy bag. She invited the family to a chicken dinner that she was preparing for us, and to come over after work.

My mother had a scheduled appointment to see her doctor about her high blood pressure. He wanted to prescribe another type of medication for her. This would be the last time he would see my mother alive.

Josie was home with Erica and Andrew when she received a phone call from my father telling her that Concha had taken a pill and was not feeling well. Josie rushed to my parents' house and immediately went into the bedroom where my mother was in bed. Josie asked her what happened. She told Josie that the doctor had changed her medication, and she was not feeling well. She said the medication was on top of the microwave. Josie picked up the bottles of pills and asked her which one she had taken. Josie read the labels on the bottles and showed my mother the pills. By this time, Canto had called 911, for he knew Concha was in serious discomfort and was having difficulty breathing.

When the paramedics arrived, Josie showed them the pills and told them that Concha had been hospitalized twice before for allergic reactions to new prescriptions and seemed to be having a reaction again to her new high blood pressure medication. The paramedics called the hospital to tell them they were transporting a 74-year-old woman and explained the situation to them.

Josie left me a note to hurry to my parents' house because my mother was very sick. As my son Phillip and I turned onto Manzanita Street, I saw a paramedic van and a police car with their lights on in front of my parents' house. We got out of the car and made our way into the house. My mother was being wheeled out on a gurney. She was pale, her face ash-white. They were taking her to Huntington Memorial Hospital.

My father was shaking all over, confused as to what was happening. He and I followed behind the ambulance to the emergency room, where they began treating her for a heart attack. This was a major mistake, since my mother was having an allergic reaction, not a heart attack. My sisters and I were told to stay in the waiting room. Shortly, the emergency nurse called us into the room where my mother was and asked what type of medication she had taken. We explained to her that the medication was the one that her doctor had prescribed to her earlier in the day and that the paramedics had taken the medication with her in the ambulance. They asked if we had the doctor's number, since they had not found it in their directory.

When I saw my mother lying on the bed, looking gravely ill, my heart sank. My father kept asking, "What's wrong with Concha? What's wrong with my wife?" All I could say was they were treating her and that she would be okay. He started to cry and hugged his wife tightly. He gave her a kiss on the cheek and said a prayer. My mother was taken to the critical care unit on the sixth floor. The emergency room began filling up with family and friends.

When my family reached the critical care unit, we noticed they were placing her in a private room. The nurse came out and told us they were going to call a cardiovascular specialist to examine her. They escorted us into a room next to hers. The curtains were drawn, and we could not see her. As we were waiting in the room, I noticed the different doctors going in to treat her. All the while, Canto kept asking questions as to what was happening to his beloved Concha.

The nurse told us they were trying to contact my mother's doctor to find out what was the antidote to this medical emergency. They would not let us go in to see her at this time. My father sank to his knees and began praying tearfully. We all prayed for my mother as we waited in the private room. My father stayed on his knees for over three hours, not once getting up. His anguish was deeply etched on his face.

At 11:30 P.M. the nurse finally came out to talk with us about our mother. She said she was sorry, but the doctors didn't think they would be able to save her. Her lungs were continuing to fill with fluid, the nurse said, and they could not reverse this. She told us to go to our mother's bedside to say our final goodbyes. They had not yet pronounced her dead, but we could tell she was near death. We had to get my father up from his knees and take him into the room to say his farewell.

My mother was not breathing on her own but was connected to a respirator. She was surrounded by tubes and wires hooked up to her. I began crying and lay on her bed. Everyone in the room wept. This was the most difficult thing I had ever witnessed in my life. I had to say goodbye to my mother one last time. How could this be happening? I had just talked with her on the phone a few hours earlier.

My father seemed to be in shock, bewildered as to what was happening to his beloved wife. We all said our final goodbyes and left the room. The doctor came over to us and said she had suffered an anaphylactic shock reaction to the medication she had taken earlier in the day. He also told us they had been unable to contact her doctor. Our mother passed away at 12:01 A.M. on November 19, and we requested an autopsy.

≈≈≈

In Deep Grief

My sisters spent the night at our father's house. We planned to meet the next day to discuss caring for our father on Manzanita Street. Josie and I went home to our house in Pasadena, where my Uncle Frankie was watching our children for us. We had to tell him what had just happened to Concha. He could not believe the devastating news.

It was very difficult trying to sleep that night. Josie and I tossed and turned, devastated that my mother had passed away so suddenly. I kept asking her about my mom's death. How could something like this happen? What were we going to do with my father? We knew he needed 24-hour care. We had so many questions and no answers. The following morning, Josie and I decided to move in with Canto to take care of him.

Within a few days, when reality set in for my father that his beloved wife had passed away, Canto suffered a stroke. We woke up to a loud thumping sound, rushed to Canto's bedroom, and found him on the floor. He was unable to stand on his own feet; the right side of his face was contorted. He was trying to speak, but was totally incoherent. Canto was dazed, confused, and so bewildered. He wanted to know where Concha was. We sat him on the bed and tried to comfort him.

She had been his eyes for so many years, and now those eyes were gone forever. Never would he be able to see through the lenses of his lifelong love. Not only was his heart broken and shattered, he had lost the only person in the world to see for him and make his world safe.

I phoned my father's doctor and explained his symptoms to him. I was told to bring Canto into Saint Luke's Hospital immediately, and he was quickly admitted. After we signed the necessary papers, the treating physician came out and told us that he had suffered a massive stroke that had paralyzed the right side of his body. He was fortunate to be alive. The death of his wife had been a tremendous shock to his heart. Canto would be hospitalized for an undetermined amount of time.

My sisters and I met at Cabot and Sons Funeral Home to plan our mother's funeral: a rosary on Tuesday, Catholic Mass on Wednesday, and burial in Glendora, California following the mass. My father was unable to attend the funeral, since he was still in the hospital. When we visited him there afterward, his speech was still impaired, and the right side of his face was still stricken. His spirits were very low. He asked about Concha again, wondering when she was coming to see him. I'm not quite sure my dad understood the enormous loss we had all just endured. We tried to clarify for him that his wife of a lifetime had died, but his brain could not let him understand.

I was still in a state of shock myself and had not been able to sleep properly. All my thoughts were with my mother. I read a poem to her that day which was part of the eulogy at Saint Andrew's Church. I can still remember looking out over the congregation, awed at the immense crowd, at all the people who had come to mourn alongside us. While I was reading the poem, I looked up and felt my mother's presence.

After the burial that day, our family, extended family, and friends gathered at Irene's house for the wake. This was a celebration of life for our mother. Everyone shared personal stories of her. Again, I began weeping. I missed her so much. I just could not accept her loss. She was the guiding force of the family. My father's eyes were darkened once again, forever.

CHAPTER 22:
Farewell to a Champion

We lived with my father for about a year when Josie and I decided to move back to our home. My father wanted to continue living in his home, and we were able to find a care provider to move in with him.

After the death of my mother, my father was never the same. He was chronically depressed and wanted to be with his wife Concha. We tried getting him involved in the gym, but he never seemed to have the desire to start training fighters again. My father's spirit died the same night my mother passed away.

The following year in August 1989, Joey Olivera and I decided to promote a boxing show at the Elks Club in Pasadena. Canto had made a full recovery from his stroke. We were happy to have him as an advisor to the show. This would be the last and final promotion for the Crown City Boxing Stables.

In 1993, five years after Concha's passing, we decided it was best for our father to move in with my sister Irene in Glendora. It was time to sell the property on Manzanita Street. Before the property was sold, Canto told me to dismantle the gym and to keep all the equipment, including the ring apron and boxing posters. He said everything must go; there would be no more Crown City Boxing Stables. That was his final wish regarding the gym.

Canto moved in with Irene and her children: Jerry Jr. (Jay), John, Jimmy, Laura, and Jesse. Irene hired Eleanor, one of our cousins, to take care of our father while she worked at Duarte High School. Eleanor was an older lady, energetic and bright. My father truly enjoyed living with Irene because, he said, she reminded him of Concha in her personality, her mannerisms, and her deliciously cooked meals. He also enjoyed all the attention from her children, who made him feel welcome and comfortable. The children would often take Canto on walks around the neighborhood. For her part, Irene sincerely enjoyed having him live with her and liked watching him shadow box every morning. She considered him hilarious to have around. He enjoyed going to all the family gatherings with Irene's family, and his brothers and friends visited him at Irene's house.

Gloria, Canto's firstborn child, my eldest sister, was one of the most stalwart, loyal family members toward Canto, not just during Canto's good years, but also—and especially so—when our father became frail and in greater need of care. Her devotion and compassion for our father never wavered. After our mother died, she became an even greater factor in our family unit, being the centerpiece of almost all our family celebrations: birthdays, Christmas, New Year's, weekend barbecues for family and friends, and all the rallying we did around our father to make him feel safe and loved.

Since Gloria lived only one block away from Irene, it was possible for my two sisters to "tag team" their care of Canto. It must have been very comforting to my father to have both his daughters close at hand, literally and figuratively. As for my part, though my wife Josie and I lived a little farther away in Glendora, we made sure that we took my father to local parks to get him outdoors in the fresh air as much as we could, and we visited him frequently. Canto had sacrificed so much to provide a safe, loving environment for us, his children, throughout our lives. Now, in his waning years, it was our turn to shower him with attention and our devotion.

Canto's only absent child was my brother Bobby, his firstborn son, who was living in a group home in Duarte very close to Irene's home in these years. Bobby was not as independent and as free with his time as the rest of us were, so this precluded him from spending time with his father and us. Canto understood the constraints Bobby was enduring, and Canto was grateful simply to be physically close to Bobby. This made Canto happy. Sadly, however, in 1996, Bobby was taken to San Gabriel Hospital complaining of chest pains and with a body temperature of 103. He was admitted into the critical care unit, where he stayed while tests were being conducted. Two days later, Bobby passed away due to congestive heart failure, leaving behind three children: Eddie, Sandra, and Doreen.

❦❦

The Final Bell

After several years, Eleanor was unable to take care of Canto, and our family was unable to find a replacement caregiver. Irene worked fulltime and couldn't care for our father during the day, so we placed him in a board and care facility in La Puente. While in their care one day, my father fell out of his wheelchair and fractured his left hip.

We wanted the best care for him, so we placed him in a convalescent hospital in Glendora. We regularly visited him and spent precious hours reminiscing about the old times. He enjoyed talking about his boxing matches with Speedy Dado, Midget Wolgast, Young Tommy, Pancho Villa, Young Sport, and Foster Manalo. He even remembered getting ready to fight Panama Al Brown for the world's title in Paris, France. Yes, we would talk about his last fight with Hilo Hernandez, which was supposed to be a tune-up fight. It turned out to be his final fight and his last sight.

My father, like others his age, began to experience dementia and other physical problems. His hip was not healing well, but he was too old to have surgery. Our father enjoyed homemade food we took to him, and having coffee and sweet bread on the patio with us. He was joyous when family members visited him, especially his brothers, Benny, Julio, and Frankie, and his sisters Artie and Alice. Family was always the most important thing in life to him.

I was teaching on Monday morning, November 29, 1999, at the Valley View Elementary School when I received a call from the office summoning me right away. I was told that the principal was going to cover my class. I instructed my class to continue what they were doing, and I would be back shortly. Walking down the hallway to the office, I noticed Irene walking toward me, crying, with a look of utter sadness.

"Daddy is dead," she said simply. "He just died of natural causes."

We hugged each other and cried our hearts out.

❧❧

I will always miss my father with a heavy heart. He was my role model, and I owe everything I am today to him and mother. The wisdom and guidance they gave me in my life made a big difference in helping me attain my own personal success. Despite his blindness, my father had an uncanny way of understanding people and their needs. He loved his family immensely. We were always number one.

He also defied conventional wisdom. Many would expect that he'd be bitter about boxing, about this sport that had blinded him forever and diminished his capacity in many ways. But the fact is that my father never turned his back on the sport he loved so much. Instead, he channeled the joy and pride he had felt each time he stepped into a ring, gloved and ready for battle, into the joy and fulfillment he felt in training, coaching, and nurturing the youth and young adults of Pasadena to be the best they could each time *they* stepped onto the canvas.

My father gave most of his life and heart to the sport of boxing. His Crown City Boxing Stables tasted the thrill of a state championship through the success of Joey Olivera and also tasted many victories through the successes of boxers—young, adult, small, and heavyweight—through all the decades of bouts.

Canto would often say: "After all, there are many things in life more important than one's eyesight. What a person feels is more important than what he sees."

And, as Rick Lozano, a KABC television newscaster, once said about Canto "TNT" Robledo: "Although sightless, he is not without vision."

EPILOGUE:
Posthumous Honors

The spirit and legacy of Canto "TNT" Robledo lives on through all the Robledo family and friends. One of Canto's nephews, Shannon Robledo, has founded the Canto Robledo Foundation, which sponsors fundraising events in Canto's honor. All proceeds are donated to the local boxing clubs to provide them with new boxing equipment.

Joey "the Pasadena Kid" Olivera continues Canto's legacy by teaching boxing to youths to instill Canto's dedication, perseverance, and determination. Much like Canto, Joey is helping combat juvenile delinquency. Canto led by example by routinely exercising and modeling a healthy lifestyle, similar goals Joey continues with his trainees.

In 2005, the California Boxing Hall of Fame posthumously inducted Canto as the only blind manager and trainer of amateur and professional fighters in the United States. My entire family attended the ceremony, and we accepted the award on behalf of our father. Other honorees that year included Jim Healy, Paul Gonzales, and Jack Johnson.

In July 2010, the Pasadena Mexican-American History Association unveiled the Canto Robledo Living Memorial, "Canto and Kids," a bas-relief wall memorial located at the Villa Parke Neighborhood Community Center in Pasadena. Artist Steven Harpst designed and built this memorial. Our family was delighted that respected local visionaries were present—Victor Gordo, Vice Mayor of Pasadena; President Manuel Contreras; Sandie Mejía, Chairperson of the Pasadena Mexican-American History Association; and Rachel Heredia, Secretary, as well as others—along with a devoted, loyal fan base of Canto and his boxers. My guiding force, my wife Josie, was also present and a great source of joy that day.

In July 2010, Canto was posthumously awarded the Joe Louis Humanitarian Award from Chief Boxing Inspector Joey Olmos on behalf of the World Boxing Hall of Fame. Olmos, as Chief Inspector of the California State Athletic Commission for more than 20 years, selected Canto Robledo as recipient of this award in recognition of Canto's many years of contributions to the community. The Joe Louis Humanitarian Award was established in 1981, following the death of former World Heavyweight Champion Joe Louis. This award and recognition is given to those individuals who have exemplified themselves in community service. The award is a bronze medallion similar to an Olympic medal, containing a profile of Joe Louis. Some previous recipients of this honor have been Muhammad Ali, Ken Norton, Bobby Chacon, Nelson Mandela, and Danny "Little Red" Lopez.

In April 2017, the Pasadena Sports Hall of Fame and Tournament of Roses inducted Canto for his contributions to Pasadena's sports legacy. The event was held at the prestigious Langham Hotel in San Marino, California. The afternoon ceremony was dubbed "A Champion's Toast." Canto's legacy in bringing honor to the community has thus been placed alongside the achievements in that category by such greats as Jackie and Mack Robinson.

Finally, at the time of this writing, Canto "TNT" Robledo is scheduled for induction into the West Coast Boxing Hall of Fame on September 30, 2018, at the Garland Hotel Event Center in North Hollywood, California. The president of the organization is Rick Farris, a former professional boxer and the author of this book's Introduction.

The embracing of Canto Robledo by Pasadena, the greater California community, and the boxing community in general was, and continues to be, one of the greatest sources of happiness and gratitude on the part of our large Robledo family and extended family members. The opportunities for success that Canto was afforded by many promoters, managers, fight officials, stadium owners, fellow boxers, and others in boxing enabled Canto to rise out of poverty and anonymity and to be in a position to aid others. His mission in life—making life better for others by helping and teaching—was a possible dream because of the immense network of supporters and their outpouring of love and loyalty to him. Our family thanks all the people in Canto's world for having done this.

ACKNOWLEDGMENTS

I would like to acknowledge my mother, Concha Jimenez Robledo, who was a guiding force for our family and a true light and inspiration for my father, Canto Robledo. My siblings—Gloria Robledo Romero, Robert "Bobby" Robledo, and Irene Robledo Tellez—have all been instrumental in the making of this book and to the success of carrying on our family legacy of perseverance, hard work, dedication, determination, and a passion for life.

My endless gratitude to my beautiful wife, Josie Robledo, whom I met 38 years ago in Pasadena, California in a genuine case of "love at first sight." We married and soon started our family: three wonderful children, Erica, Phillip, and Andrew "Bam Bam" Robledo. We are proud of them and our lovely granddaughter, Marysa. Josie's faith and confidence in me as I worked hard on this book enabled me to keep moving forward. My family's unwavering support was my rock throughout this project.

This book is filled with the true accounts and fascinating stories shared with me over the years by the first generation of the Robledo family in the United States, birthed by my grandparents, Canto's parents, Felipe Robledo, Sr. and Soledad Cimental Robledo. Canto told me many stories as I was growing up, and for that, I'm forever grateful. In the past few years, as I wrote this book, I relied on the memories of Canto's surviving sisters: Artie (Aurelia) Nunnery, Alice (Alicia) Mercado, and Canto's brothers—Manuel, Benny (Basilio), Julio, Sever (Severino), Philip (Felipe), Joe (Jose), and Frankie (Francisco) Robledo. This first generation of elders forged the way in America for the rest of us, with their grit, fortitude, hard work, and determination to flourish. The newer generations of extended family and in-laws continued our family devotion, such as Arthur Romero Sr., who built the Crown City Boxing Stables.

I also thank some great champions who have supported the legacy of Canto "TNT" Robledo: the West Coast Boxing Hall of Fame President, Rick Farris; California Boxing Hall of Fame President, Don Frazier; Los Angeles boxing promoter, Don Chargin; the late Joey

Olmos, Chief Athletic Boxing Inspector; Steve Harpst, sculptor and artist for his design of "Canto and Kids" Bronze Living Wall Memorial located at the Villa Parke Community Center, in Pasadena, California; Los Angeles County Supervisor Michael Antonovich, for Canto's recognition award in 1988, acknowledging Canto's untiring efforts in the training and discipline of young boxers and for furthering the sport of boxing, especially with our youth.

Others whom I deeply thank are the City of Pasadena; Shannon Robledo, great-nephew and founder of the Canto Robledo Foundation; Sergeant Shannon Robledo, South Pasadena Police Department; the Pasadena Mexican History Association for their enormous support; Jimmy Lennon, Jr., professional boxing ring announcer; Danny "Little Red" Lopez, World Featherweight Champion; Jack Mosley, father and trainer of Sugar Shane Mosley, Super Welterweight and World Lightweight Champion; Joey Olivera, California State Lightweight Champion; Ray Mercado, Pasadena Crown City Boxing Stables trainer and cornerman; Luis Tirado, Pasadena Crown City Boxing Stables trainer and cornerman; and to the countless young men and women who came to train, exercise, and learn the sport of boxing through the vision and leadership of Canto "TNT" Robledo.

A special thank you goes out to Peter Embody for his time, effort and assistance in completing this project. Finally, a huge thank you to my editor and publisher, Dr. Thelma T. Reyna, of Golden Foothills Press, for making this dream come true.

I am thankful for my father's guiding spirit while writing this book and for all the blessings the Lord has bestowed on our family and friends.

--Joseph C. Robledo

APPENDIX A:
Articles About Canto "TNT" Robledo

The following articles appeared in various publications during Canto's career, from the beginning till his death. (In some of these early articles, Canto Robledo was referred to as "Canto Robleto.") These are representative samples of the extensive acknowledgment and publicity Canto received in his life. The information below should be helpful to his fans in accessing these archives, where the articles can be read in their entirety.

Friday, June 28, 1929
Pasadena Independent Star News
"Muscle Bound"
By Fredrick Graham

Telegram Message 9-27-1929, Western Union
Pasadena, California, September 27, 1929- Canto Robleto Mexican Flyweight defeated the Filipino veteran, Foster Manalo in an eight round main event here last night.

October 22, 1929
Pasadena Independent Star News
"Canto to Star in Main Event Thursday"
Staff Writer

Thursday, October 31, 1929
Pasadena Star News
"Canto Robleto Fights Tonight in Effort to Extend Winning Streak. Robleto Makes Initial Main Event Showing"
Staff Writer

Friday, May 30, 1930
Pasadena Star News
"Great Boxing Show Given at Arena. Every bout Exciting on Card Last Night. Canto has Arrived as Fighter"
Staff Writer

Thursday, June 12, 1930
Pasadena Independent Star News
"Canto Will Meet Dado. Flyweights will Battle in Main Event at Arena Tomorrow Night"
Staff Writer

Friday, June 13, 1930
Pasadena Star News
"Robleto And Dado Fight To Draw. Local Boy Makes Great Showing at Arena"
Staff Writer

Friday, August 9, 1930
The Los Angeles Times – www.Newspapers.com
"Wolgast Defeats Robleto Easily in Hollywood Go"
[Unlisted author]

Friday, December 5, 1931
Oakland Tribune Sports – www.Newspapers.com
"Robleto Awarded Decision in San Francisco"
[Unlisted author]

Sunday, December 6, 1931
The Oakland Tribune Sports – www.Newspapers.com
"Wolgast is Signed with Canto Robleto"
[Unlisted author]

November 1950
Pasadena Star News
"ORV Mohler Memorial Honors Canto Robledo"
By Mannie Piñeda

February 1951
Pasadena Sports Scene
"Sportingly Yours: You Can See for Yourself Tonight"
By Mannie Piñeda

August 7, 1952
Pasadena Star News
"On an Undefeated Champion"
By Bob Shafer, Sports Editor

April 25, 1954
Pasadena Star News
"Hail the Conquering Hero"
By Bob Shafer

Friday, June 17, 1955
Los Angeles Examiner – www.Newspapers.com
"To the Point: The Blind Man Who Teaches Boxing"
By Al Santoreo, Sports Editor

Wednesday, September 26, 1956
Independent Star News
"Canto Honored by His Peers: Canto Robledo Honored at Boxing
Writers Fete"
By Mannie Piñeda

Saturday, November 3, 1956
Independent Star news
"Canto Holds Benefit Dance for Unfortunate Kids"
By Robert Smith, Sports Editor

Saturday, August 23, 1958
Pasadena Independent Star News
"Finals Reached by Joe Robledo"
Staff Writer

Saturday August 30, 1958
Pasadena Independent Star News
"Robledo Wins Title"
Staff Writer

Sunday, September 14, 1958
Pasadena Independent Star News
"Canto Robledo Slated for Top Honors at Fair"
By Mannie Piñeda

Friday, May 16, 1959
Pasadena Independent Star News
"Top Amateur Ring Card Slated at Muir Friday"
Staff Writer

Sunday, May 17, 1959
Pasadena Independent Star News
"Unselfish Canto Dreams of Champ"
By Wells Twombly

Tuesday, December 15, 1959
Pasadena Independent Star News
"Man of Many Missions"
Staff Writer

Tuesday, September 22, 1964
Pasadena Independent Star News
"Tragedy 'Cornered' Robledo, but He Came Back Swinging"
By Don Pickard

Sunday, January 30, 1966
Los Angeles Times
"Blind Trainer 'Sees' His Fighters"
By John Allan

April 1968
Boxing Illustrated –Ringside News
"A Man of Great Vision"
By William O'Neill

Sunday, October 7, 1973
Pasadena Independent Star News
"Blind Boxing Instructor"
By Gary Libman, Associated Press Writer

October 1974
The Ring
"Up and Down Old Broadway"
By Sam Taub

November 20, 1980
Q-Vo
"Canto Robledo: Warrior of the Ring"
By Gloria González-Roth

Sunday, July 13, 1986
The Los Angeles Times – www.Newspapers.com
"Fall in Line"
By Jim Murray

October 14, 1987
Pasadena Star News – www.Newspapers.com
"Olivera Gains State Title, but Appeal May Overturn"
By Ramon Álvarez

Tuesday, November 30, 1999
Pasadena Star News – www.Newspapers.com
"Boxer, Trainer Canto Robledo Dies"
By Steve Hunt, Sports Editor

APPENDIX B:

Canto Robleto (Robledo): Lifetime Boxing Record

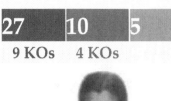

27 — 9 KOs | 10 — 4 KOs | 5

global ID	44705
role	boxer
bouts	42
rounds	236
KOs	21%
status	inactive
alias	TNT/Nitroglicerina
nationality	USA
debut	1929-06-29
division	bantamweight
residence	Pasadena, California, USA

Canto Robleto, bantamweight from Pasadena, California

[Information from http://www.boxrec.com with correction made in 2018 by the Robledo family regarding total wins, which was listed incorrectly online.]

ABOUT THE AUTHOR

Photo by Andrew Robledo

Joseph C. Robledo was born and raised in Pasadena, CA, the adopted home of his iconic father Canto and the birthplace of Canto's famous Crown City Boxing Stables. Joseph's life was interwoven with boxing, as he was close to his father and an integral member of Canto's team in and out of the ring. Joseph was an amateur boxer as an adolescent and won the Junior Golden 65-Pound Novice Division Championship in 1956, when he was also named Most Outstanding Fighter in the tournament. His overall ring record was 27-3-1 by the time he stopped boxing to focus on his academic goals.

A native son of California, Joseph attended local schools; taught in the Oak Grove, Pasadena, and Duarte school districts; coached various school teams; and was an adjunct professor at Pasadena City College and California State University, Los Angeles. He received a BA Degree in Physical Education from Cal State LA and an MA in Physical Education from Azusa Pacific University.

He recently retired after teaching for 38 years. Joseph also served as an Athletic Inspector in boxing sanctions for the State of California.

For Readers' Notes